The Biscuit Girls

The Biscuit Girls

Hunter Davies

EBURY
PRESS

3 5 7 9 10 8 6 4 2

Published in 2014 by Ebury Press, an imprint of Ebury Publishing
A Random House Group company

Copyright © Hunter Davies 2014

Photos on pages 11, 75, 102, 117, 187 and 213 © their subject. Photos on
pages 263, 271,281, 289, 309 and 318 © Hunter Davies. Photos on pages
58 and 170 © Tullie House Trust, Carlisle. Photos on pages 31, 86, 183 and
341 courtesy of Cumbria Image Bank www.cumbriaimagebank.org.uk

The Random House Group Limited Reg. No. 954009

Addresses for companies within the Random House Group can be found at
www.randomhouse.co.uk

A CIP catalogue record for this book is available from the British Library

The Random House Group Limited supports the Forest Stewardship
Council® (FSC®), the leading international forest-certification organisation.
Our books carrying the FSC label are printed on FSC®-certified paper. FSC is
the only forest-certification scheme supported by the leading environmental
organisations, including Greenpeace. Our paper procurement policy
can be found at www.randomhouse.co.uk/environment

Printed and bound by CPI Group (UK) Ltd, Croydon, CR0 4YY

ISBN 9780091957643

To buy books by your favourite authors and register for offers visit
www.randomhouse.co.uk

Contents

Introduction

In the 1950s, when my twin sisters Marion and Annabelle were at the Margaret Sewell School in Carlisle and my wife Margaret was at the Carlisle and County High School for Girls, teachers would warn all the girls that if they didn't stick at their lessons they would end up as 'cracker packers'.

Everybody in Carlisle knew what that meant – and still do, for the phrase and the activity continues to this day. It referred to the women workers on the production line at Carr's biscuit factory, standing there all day, packing crackers. Who on earth would want to do that sort of menial, tedious, repetitive job? That was the fairly unsubtle message, not to say dreaded warning to get a grip, get your head down, pass those exams, get some proper qualifications and then you will be off, free and independent, not condemned to a life of factory work.

But of course for many unskilled, unschooled workers, Carr's was looked upon as a good job, attracting women from all over the surrounding area. Ethel Bragg, the mother of Melvyn Bragg (the writer and broadcaster, now Lord Bragg of Wigton), worked at Carr's from 1930 to 1931, coming in each day on the bus. She died in 2012, aged ninety-five.

'My mother was a cracker packer for about a year,' so Melvyn told me, 'until her name came up for a job in her home town at Redmaynes, the clothing factory, where she made buttonholes until she married in 1938 when, as was the custom, she was fired for the offence of matrimony. She was very happy working at Carr's. It was one of the very few jobs available for girls who left school at fourteen and what used to be delightfully called "without any qualifications". She used to get the bus from Wigton into Carlisle and get off at Trinity Church – now gone – which was the bus stop opposite the biscuits works. At home, we always bought Carr's water biscuits.'

Factory workers have always had a bad press. In all towns, in all industrial nations, at all times, since it all began, there has always been one factory, one sort of job which has become a term of contempt or of pity, about which local people either sneer or feel sorry. Charles Dickens scared the souls off all right-thinking Victorians by his memories of sticking labels on bottles of shoe polish in Warren's boot blacking factory. Today we have dreadful tales of sweat shops in China and south-east Asian clothes factories.

When Margaret went on to Oxford on an Open Scholarship, and got her name on the Honours Board in the school hall, she used to come home to Carlisle and say she would have learned more about real life had she gone to work at the Carr's factory.

Obviously, aged nineteen, she knew little about real life, at Carr's or elsewhere, and it was a bit of bravado. And yet she knew there was something about these women whom she had met, had listened to when growing up on the Raffles council estate, whose lives and opinions and experiences were just as valid as anyone with a fancy education or more privileged background.

In the 1950s, women had already been packing crackers at Carr's for well over a hundred years, in a factory producing biscuits that dates back to 1837, which boasted that it was the home of biscuits. Many of them had served there for the whole of their working lives, loyal and proud to have worked for Carr's, a benevolent family firm, some of them receiving long-service awards after clocking up forty-five years. The workers must have known that they were engaging in a meaningful if modest task, their minds probably miles away while they were silently, automatically packing crackers that would be dispatched around the world. For were not Carr's Table Water Biscuits known and enjoyed in all the corners of the globe? So they were being told in the company magazine, the *Topper Off*.

Many years later, in 1997, Margaret published a book about the history of Carr's, *Rich Desserts and Captain's Thin*.* The title is a bit of a mouthful – they were two of Carr's famous early biscuits.

In her book, she was dealing with the early years, from 1831 to 1931, and it was mainly about the Carr family, following them down the generations. It won a prize and sold well and naturally I am greatly indebted to it for background information. At the time, though, I remember her moaning about the lack of letters from the main participants, about the problem of finding any colour or personal details or about real life on the factory floor. But it was meant to be a serious, quasi-academic study, of a pre-war family business dynasty. It did not concern itself with the workers, or the post-war decades. Which is what I have now decided to attempt.

What was life really like for the ordinary women factory workers, the ones who packed the biscuits? How did they stand it? Were they just doing it for the money? How hard was it? Were they happy, accepting or merely resigned? Or was it their home and personal life, outside their factory life, that really mattered to them?

There is some decent oral history of what it was like be a Carr's factory worker, tape-recorded interviews that cover the period back to the First World War. They

---

* Margaret Foster, *Rich Desserts and Captain's Thin* (Chatto & Windus, London: 1997)

were made in the 1950s and again in the 1980s, part of that sudden interest in capturing working-class, local history, which sprang up after the last war and is today available in most local library and records offices.

It is noticeable, in the Carlisle archives, that members of the Carr family, so important in the city and the county for many decades, were not interviewed. It was the ordinary workers that archivists wanted to capture in those post-war years.

I have listened to and read many of these oral accounts, and found them all fascinating – but I have not used them here, except for a couple of examples. For, while they are rich on the inter-war or immediate post-war years, they are stories of women now dead, and the task I set myself was to capture the stories of women still alive today, who started in the 1940s, 1950s and 1960s, and some of whom were still working at the factory up until the last couple of years. For life at Carr's, and at similar factories all over the country, all over the world, still goes on, though the number of factory workers in the UK is roughly half of what it was in the immediate post-war years.

One problem with oral history, fascinating though it can be, is that it is not proactive. The oral historian's tape recorder records, content to receive what it is being told. Oral historians are essentially archivists, not seeing it as their job to cross-examine, counter or comment.

The problem with the opposite, journalistic approach is that while the interviewer might properly engage, stir up and drag out, he or she often has an agenda, even if it just their own personal interests and concerns, which can slant or distort the end result, highlighting certain aspects, minimising others.

I like to think I have let the six women who tell their story here talk naturally, as they wanted to, allowing their own memories to flow freely, but also making them try hard to remember feelings and events, fashions and entertainments, local and national, that they all have lived through. I am roughly the same age as them, and my childhood home was Carlisle, so this helped me to focus them, and jog their memories of times and places, without, I hope, trying to make them fit any of my preconceptions or prejudices.

However, the book is not just about the lives of six women. It is equally a slice of recent social history, about events and changes in Carlisle, most of which were going on in Britain and the Western world at large. As we progress through their lives, at work and at home, I have tried to put their personal experiences in a broader context, for those who might have forgotten or never knew when exactly it was that the Pill came in, beehives were fashionable, when the horrors of the Eleven Plus happened, or when sales of the first council houses became possible. Carlisle might be a fairly remote town, where things have usually arrived late, but since the war, all of us still alive and of a certain age have lived through and experienced much the same changes in conditions, fashions and attitudes. Even if we didn't realise it at the time.

Along with the general social history, as reflected in the lives of our six women, there is also a more specialist history – the history of biscuits, and of Carr's in particular. Biscuits have had a role, a bit part, in all our personal lives these last 150 years, in wars and in famines, peace times and at work. Few there are who have not longed, in good or bad times, for a Nice Cup of Tea and a Biscuit. Yet, strangely enough, there is no book about the history of biscuits. There are individual histories of the leading firms, such as Carr's or Huntley & Palmers, but I have failed so far to find a general history that covers the whole story of biscuits, right back to the beginning.

I found the six women whose stories are told here through a Carr's pensioners club for women who had retired from the factory. I talked to a group, explained the project, made it clear I wanted to know about their personal lives, not just their work at the factory, and asked for volunteers. I thought they shouldn't be all of exactly the same age, but a broad range of ages so they would have a span of experience to share.

I had to resist the temptation to draw parallels or

proclaim trends, but I think they are a fairly typical sample of post-war working women: ending up spinsters or married, some fit and healthy, others suffering failing health having faced the same sort of problems of most modern families, from divorce to drug-related deaths. As we shall see, some preferred to stick to working on the line, whereas others discovered they had different ambitions. The six in the book are aged between sixty and eighty. Four of the six were born pre-war, so have vivid wartime memories. Two were born post-war, growing up in the sixties, reacting to all the new social changes, reflecting the modern notions of female entitlement and ambition. I did have a seventh, but she dropped out, having originally agreed. During my first proper meeting with her at her own home, discussing again the point of the book and what I would be asking, she changed her mind. She had been involved in a messy divorce. The details were not secret, known to her family and friends, but it had all been so awful that she didn't want to relive the experience through talking about it.

Factory work of the sort they experienced is changing, and will change as more automated machinery comes in, so in one sense they are period pieces, the end of the line. But there will always be some sort of industry somewhere in the world taking advantage of the sweat of women who see little alternative.

At the time of writing, the six women were all alive, each living in their own homes, enjoying their retirement after what has been by normal standards an exceedingly hard life. Their names are real, as real as the lives they have lived, and nothing has been changed. I can't thank each of them enough for their time and their memories, their thoughts and feelings.

Hunter Davies
Loweswater, Cumbria, 2014

Carr's advertisement from 1950s

Chapter 1

Ivy

Ivy aged fourteen in the school netball team

'Ivy, go and see if anyone is in the lavatory, will you, pet?' said Ivy's grandmother.

So four-year-old Ivy toddled off down the little lane behind her grandmother's house in Brook Street, an old Victorian terrace which had communal wash houses behind and a single outside lavatory, shared by all. Ivy was a stumpy, broad-shouldered little girl, always cheerful, always smiling, always wanting to please.

The year was 1937. Ivy and her parents and her big brother Tommy had recently moved into a new council house not far away in Dalton Avenue. Her grandmother's house had one room downstairs, which was the living room, plus a pantry, and two bedrooms upstairs. They had gas mantles for lighting and open coal fire for heat, on which they made toast and boiled a kettle for tea.

Ivy loved going to visit her grandmother, helping in any way she could, even though the house was poky and cramped with very few amenities, compared with her family's new council house. The dustman could drive right into the backyard at her grandmother's, where the wash house and lavatory were, and if they were in a good mood, and not in a hurry, they would give little Ivy a lift round to the front of her grandmother's house. Brook Street has long since been knocked down, considered one of the city's poorer areas, not far from the old industrial slums of Caldewgate.

On this particular day, the lavatory was empty, so when Ivy rushed back with the good news, her grand-mother grabbed the big iron key on a long piece of string and made a dash for it. And got there in time, before anyone else had spotted the vacancy.

Ivy was born in her grandmother's house, hence her affection for it, on 2 August 1933, and was named Ivy Emma. Emma was chosen by her grandmother. Growing up, Ivy always hated the name Emma and tried to keep it secret. Now, eighty years later, it has become fashionable again.

'My mother went home to her own house to have me, which was normal at the time. My brother Tommy, seven years older, was born there as well. Of course we had hospitals in Carlisle in the 1930s, but I suppose you felt safe in your own house, back with your mam.

'My grandmother's house might have been fairly primitive, but the wash house was excellent. They had this wood-fired boiler that heated the water so hot you couldn't touch it. In fact, my mam used to take all our washing there. She could never get the boiler hot enough in our own house.'

Her grandmother had been a factory worker in her youth, at Buck's, a clothing factory, known for its shirts. Her husband Isaac, twelve years older, was a labourer in the Hudson Scott factory, famous for its tins, especially biscuit tins. Ivy's father was a labourer and worked at 14 MU, an RAF maintenance unit, across the other side of Carlisle.

Ivy's house was on the Raffles estate, and had an indoor lavatory and a bathroom. The Raffles estate had been created as a model council estate, with nothing too good for the workers. The movement for better housing had started after the First World War. 'The only adequate solution to the housing question,' said the King's Speech in 1919, 'is to build houses specifically for the poor.'

The government made grants and Carlisle City Council was proud that it was one of the first local authorities to snap up the subsidies. Their first council houses opened in 1922. The earliest of many new council estates on the edge of the city was at Long-sowerby and the council lashed out on good building materials and provided a variety of styles, some with bay windows and parlours, proper bathrooms and indoor lavatories. They were so desirable that it was found that many white-collar workers, who in theory could have managed a mortgage to buy their own house, were rushing to get on the council-renting list. In 1926 the council purchased ninety-eight acres at Raffles, a mile to the west of the city centre, and the city architect Percy Dalton was told to fit in as many houses as he could, and also provide a new park, shops, a church and other amenities. The Raffles estate did not have the variety enjoyed at Longsowerby, and most of the houses were more basic, without bay windows and front parlours, but they were still well built and modern and nearer the middle of the town, handy for workers in Caldewgate, where the Carr's factory was situated. This time the council managed to restrict the tenants to industrial, blue-collar workers, many of them rehoused from the slums in Caldewgate. When they were nearing completion, young families would walk round Raffles on Sunday afternoon to admire the new houses and all the greenery and new shops. The average weekly rent in 1930 was six shillings, out of an average industrial wage of two pounds, three shillings and tuppence.

When completed, the Raffles estate contained 2,352 houses. New council estates were still being built in Carlisle after the war and by the 1950s, over 60 per cent of Carlisle's population lived in council houses, a high proportion but in line with most other towns in the UK. Ivy's council house in Raffles, where she grew up, was in Dalton Avenue, named after Raffles's architect.

At the age of five, Ivy started at the local primary school, Ashley Street. For some reason, her mother had not signed all the appropriate forms, so on the first day, when she took little Ivy along, she was immediately called into the office, leaving Ivy all alone, telling her to sit still and not cause any trouble.

'I did want to cry, with my mother rushing off so quickly and leaving me, but I managed to hold it back. I was sitting in exactly the same spot when she came back. But that was me. Never any trouble. I went through my whole school career causing no trouble, doing exactly what the teachers said, hardly saying much. Made up for later, like. Now I never stop talking.

'I tried my best, but I wasn't clever, never have been. I don't know anything, really. When the teacher asked a question and we all put our hands, I would dread her asking me. So if she walked down the aisles and looked as if she was going to ask me, I would slowly put my hand down again, pretending it was a mistake.'

Ivy loved reading the *Dandy* and *Beano*. Her father got the *News of the World* and the *Empire News*, but Ivy didn't read them. Just the *Sunday Post* for 'Our Wullie' and the cartoons. The *Sunday Post* was and is a Scottish paper. Ivy did not come from a Scottish family, but Carlisle has strong Scottish connections, being only ten miles from the border, hence its title the 'Border City'. Many Carlisle families at the time got the *Sunday Post*, a homely, old-fashioned family newspaper.

'I remember one day collecting for the May Queen. It was just really a party held in our street, in our close, where one girl dresses up as the May Queen in old curtains and all the boys are dressed as chimney sweeps. I was going round the local streets collecting, asking for contributions. You usually got halfpennies or pennies, if you were lucky. But this time I stopped a man and he gave me half a crown! He was American. Don't know where he had come from. Perhaps he was a soldier, as the war was on. We had a really good children's party that year. Albert, who lived opposite, his sister worked at Carr's and she got us a big tin of biscuits with the money we had collected.'

At eleven, Ivy sat the Eleven Plus, known in Carlisle as the 'Merit'. This was the exam that tested all the country's children, dividing and sorting them, not just educationally but socially and economically for the rest of their lives.

The chosen few, and in every part of the country it was only a minority, went on to a grammar school, a path that could lead the chosen ones on to university, the professions, a proper white-collar job with a career structure. The majority went on to a secondary modern or, in many cases, just stayed where they were, in the same school they had started at five. The Eleven Plus exam came in under the Butler Education Act of 1944, which also raised the school leaving age from fourteen to fifteen, though this did not come into operation till 1947.

In Carlisle, there was a three-tier system, which was what the government had planned, but most local councils ignored it, creating only two tiers, the grammar and the secondary modern. In Carlisle, the top 12.5 per cent went on to either the Carlisle Grammar School for Boys or the Carlisle and County High School for Girls. The next 12.5 per cent went to two secondary technical schools, the Creighton for Boys and the Margaret Sewell for Girls, where some of the top class could stay on till sixteen and take O levels, but neither had a sixth form. This left the 75 per cent who had failed the Eleven Plus at the bottom rung of the educational pecking order, such as Ivy's school, Ashley Street.

All over the nation, for the rest of their lives, the millions of children who sat the compulsory Eleven Plus during the thirty or so post-war years when it was in operation remember the exam hanging over them, followed by the elation of passing, or, more commonly, the disappointment of failing, feeling they were doomed, having fallen at life's first hurdle.

However, in Ivy's case, the effect was minimal. In fact she can't really remember sitting it.

'It was about six weeks afterwards, when someone in the house happened to be talking to me mam about the Eleven Plus. I piped up and said, "Oh, I sat that."

'My mother said I hadn't told her, which was probably true. It was nothing really. All I can really remember is just one question: "How many sides has a pyramid?" I looked over to see what the girl next to me had written. She had put six. So I wrote six as well. Turns out it's, eh, actually I'm still not sure, three I think.

'The Merit didn't mean a thing to me. I didn't want to go anywhere else anyway. I loved Ashley Street so much and never wanted to leave. I knew my parents could not have afforded the uniform for the high school, so that was in my mind. But really, I had no ambition in life. Never said I wanted to do this or that. Just accepted.

'I know some teachers said to some of the girls that if you don't stick in you'll end up as a cracker packer at Carr's. That didn't seem too bad to me. In our playground at Ashley Street, we could smell the sweet smell of the biscuits and chocolate and see the streams of Carr's workers going down the hill to the factory each day. We used to climb on the railings and shout at them. Oh just silly things, make remarks about their hair, or shout, "Got any broken biscuits, missus?" I thought they looked good in their overalls, very smart.'

Ivy can only remember one girl in her class who passed the Eleven Plus and went to high school, a girl who lived near her on the Raffles estate.

'Didn't do her much good. She was hardly there, always playing truant. The school inspector was forever at her house. I don't know what happened to her in the end.'

So Ivy stayed on at Ashley Street until 1948, when she was fifteen. This meant that the bulk of her school days were spent during the war years. But for a schoolgirl in Carlisle this meant little, as the city was a relatively safe place to be. Carlisle wasn't a major target for the Luftwaffe, if they knew of its existence at all. Being a remote, isolated town in the middle of a rural area in the far north-west of England with a population of 65,000 in 1948 and far away from the industrial heartlands of Lancashire, Carlisle can hardly have registered on the German radar, either metaphorically or geographically.*

Now and again the odd bomb did fall on Carlisle, or was rumoured to have fallen, and sometimes a plane

---

* The term radar was in use, having been coined in 1940 by the US navy, an acronym for radio detection and ranging.

did crash, but it was usually a German plane that had got lost on its way to or from Liverpool or Glasgow, industrial centres, which really got a pasting.

But of course the war did have a huge effect on life generally in Carlisle, as it did everywhere in the UK, with rationing, blackouts and air-raid shelters.

'We all had a gas mask which came in a cardboard box. My mam made me a sort of black bag for it, so I could carry it over my shoulder.

'At Ashley Street, we had regular air-raid drills. We all put on our gas masks and were marched through the streets to the air-raid shelters. I hated them, they were smelly and dark and filthy. We all had to crouch down inside, then we all marched back to school again. That was it.'

Ivy didn't have a shelter at home, but now and again her father made her crouch down under the kitchen table, if there was a bomb scare, such as German bombers being spotted high up in the sky, heading for the munitions' factories at Gretna.

'My mother filled the bath with water one night and got the stirrup pump ready. The idea was that she would use it to put out any fires in the house. My dad was away that night. Anyway, having filled the bath, me mam got nervous, so she grabbed my hand and we ran to Mrs Wallace's, but she wasn't in. So we ran down the street to another neighbour's and stayed there all evening with her family. My mother felt much safer with other people.'

Ivy was very excited when her grandmother started taking in evacuees, many of them around her own age, so she had new children to play with. Evacuation began right at the beginning of the Second World War. On 1 September 1939 Operation Pied Piper sprang into action and in three days 800,000 school-age children from across England were on the move. Their schools had sent parents a letter telling them to pack clean clothes for their children, plus washing material, strong walking shoes and their favourite book. At the railway stations, they were given a gas mask and food and had a label stuck on with their name, school, home address and destination. And off they went. Some were back in a few weeks. Others remained evacuated – usually somewhere in the countryside – for the duration of the war. There were other waves of evacuees during 1940, when it was thought England was going to be invaded on the south coast and during the London Blitz. In all, well over three million children were evacuated.

As a relatively safe place, Carlisle and the surrounding area was ideal for evacuees and many households took them in, if they had the space. Most of the evacuees came over from the industrial north-east but some arrived from much further away. During the war, Roedean girls' school moved up from the south and took up residence in Keswick, using the railway station and the station hotel for lessons.

Ivy is proud of how her grandmother did her bit, taking in evacuees despite having such a small house. On her bedroom wall today, Ivy has a framed certificate given to her grandmother, signed by the King, thanking her for her war effort in taking in evacuees. She is convinced it is his real signature, signed personally for her grandmother.

Carlisle had ration books, like everybody else, so new clothes were in short supply, with little choice, but like most little northern girls of the time, Ivy usually got 'dressed for Easter', meaning that was the time of the year when her mother somehow managed to buy or acquire some new clothes.

'Once I got a coat at Studholme's for Easter, which was thought a very smart shop, but that was unusual. A lot of my clothes were homemade. My grandmother made me a tartan kilt and waistcoat one Easter which I loved.'

Food rationing meant that people had to get used to making do with dried milk and dried eggs instead of the real thing. Children believed that bananas were a mythical fruit, which they were unlikely to see or taste in their lifetime.

'In a cookery lesson at school one day, I saw this tin of dried milk. I dipped my finger in it and licked it. I felt ever so guilty afterwards.

'But there was one really serious incident. Some girl had stolen a bar of soap from the cookery room. Soap was, of course, rationed during the war. The head had us all lined up in the hall and lectured us about this terrible thing some girl had done. It was a criminal offence, and she should really report it to the police, but it would bring such shame on the school that she had decided not to do that. So would the girl own up? There was silence.

'The head then had all the suspects come to her room, one by one. Eventually one split on the other one. We all knew her name. No, I'm not mentioning it. She's dead now, but I often see her sister up the street. And of course I never mention it.'

'Mother always cooked proper teas at 5.30 each evening when my father came home from work. And she always used fresh meat and fresh vegetables and we always had a pudding. Mostly it was tapioca. On Sunday we would have a roast and then leftovers on Monday. She would also make stews and broths. Each week, she would have the same sort of meal on the same day, so you would know what was coming.

'When I came home from school each day she would always give me homemade currant squares or ginger squares, just to keep me going.

'My mother shopped in the Red Stamp shop in St Nicholas and her groceries were delivered to the door.

We never had drink in the house. My father would not allow it, so we had none at all, even at Christmas.

'My father had an allotment at the bottom of the garden. We always ate all our own vegetables. He also grew raspberries and strawberries and rhubarb, but mainly his allotment was full of potatoes, carrots, onions and cabbage. I disliked onions as a child, hated them – but I liked everything else.'

Being on the whole a very good girl, and well-behaved pupil, by the time Ivy was in the top form she was chosen for the school's netball team and had been given various positions of responsibility, such as milk monitor, handing out the little bottles of milk which all children got during the war. Often the contents had turned sour by the time it was drunk, especially in winter if the bottles had arrived frozen and been put on the radiators to thaw.

Ivy's most important job was going to the post office with the savings money. Children at all schools were encouraged to save money during the war with the National Savings certificates system, all to help the war effort. Mothers would give money to their child to take to school, usually half a crown, which would buy a savings stamp and in due course a savings certificate.

'I had to take all the money to the post office each week. I never knew how much. It was in a bag. But must have been a queer lot. Good job I didn't know. I might have been scared I'd be robbed.'

In 1948, coming up for fifteen, it was time for Ivy to leave school. She had no idea what she wanted to do, and still no ambitions of any sort.

'I was still eezy ozzy, not bothered really. I would never have dreamed of asking for anything. Girls these days are asking all the time, mainly for themselves, of course, wanting this and wanting that. We would never have dreamed of asking for anything. You waited to be asked.

'There was one job I vaguely fancied at one time – and that was working in a shoe shop. That quite appealed to me. But my dad said, "You wouldn't like it if I came in to try on a pair of shoes with my sweaty feet." So I went off that.'

Carlisle is an ancient city, not perhaps as famous as some other northern cities such as York, but it has an ancient cathedral, founded in 1122, and a castle even older, begun in 1093. Mary Queen of Scots was imprisoned in Carlisle Castle in 1568, and from its battlements she is reported to have watched the locals playing football, or a form of football, one of the earliest known sightings of the glorious game.

In 1745, Bonny Prince Charlie marched on Carlisle, on his way south from Scotland to claim the English throne, taking over the city. He only got as far as Derby, on his march to London, returning through Carlisle on his ignominious retreat home.

Apart from these two famous historic incidents, Carlisle over the centuries has not featured largely in English history or in English mythology, the sort which gets passed on through the generations. In more recent decades, there are just two things most ordinary Brits tend to know about Carlisle, if, of course, they know the name, know roughly where it is, and that it is not in Wales or Scotland.

Firstly, that their little football team, Carlisle United, got into the top division of the English football league, and for a brief moment in time – 24 August 1974, to be precise – they were top of the league, having won their first three games. Then they got demoted.

The other thing they might know about it is biscuits. Not just in the UK but around the globe, many people today still know that Carr's of Carlisle produces table water biscuits. All thanks to a man called Jonathan Dodgson Carr.

In 1948 Carlisle, despite its modest size and rural isolation, was a hive of industry, as it had been throughout most of the nineteenth century, with many factories located around the middle of the town or in Caldewgate.

There was Hudson Scott, which had started out as a printing firm in 1799 but at the end of the war was a factory that produced tins. Cowans Sheldon had made cranes since 1846. Dixons, Bucks, Morton Sundour and

Fergusons, equally long established, were textile factories which employed a lot of women and girls, as did Teasdales making sweets and Carr's making biscuits.

In the centre of the town, then and now, was the ancient pink-bricked sweet little eighteenth-century town hall, but in the immediate post-war years, it always seemed clouded in a haze of industrial smoke and soot from all the chimneys. One of them, Dixon's chimney, 320 feet high, was said to be the tallest in the land when Peter Dixon opened his textile factory in 1836.

Surrounded by the noise and bustle of a busy industrial town, it was easy to forget, or at least not be aware, how ancient and historic Carlisle was, with its medieval castle and cathedral and other ancient buildings, all clustered round the heart of what was once a walled city.

Opposite the pretty town hall the council had plonked down some public lavatories, so all day people were coming in and out, while around the ancient Market Cross, beside the old town hall, where once there had been market stalls and fairs, the old cobbled square had become the town's bus terminus, with buses arriving and departing and crowds queuing up. Most people caught their bus home from work outside the old town hall. So when the main shifts ended, at two in the afternoon, six in the evening or ten at night, the workers flooded straight from the factory gates, desperate to catch their own bus home, creating huge queues that wound their way across the cobbles. Nearby were some ancient, narrow medieval lanes, known as The Lanes, which were being allowed to fall into disrepair, supposedly to be knocked down one day to make way for a new shopping precinct – which did eventually happen. It was as if the town was in disguise, clothed in shabby, dirty, workaday grime and grit, waiting for someone to rip away the façade and say, goodness, underneath you really are pretty and attractive. But this was not to happen for another few decades.

Opposite the town hall and the Market Cross was the Crown and Mitre Hotel, still Carlisle's grandest and poshest hotel, in a prime position, passed most days by most of the working or shopping population. For centuries it had been Carlisle's main coaching inn, with travellers from elsewhere in England resting before the last stage of their stage coach journey to Scotland, up to Glasgow or Edinburgh, some hundred miles or so further on.

In 1745 Bonnie Prince Charlie and his main supporters had stayed there, the landlord of the time being a Jacobite sympathiser. Sir Walter Scott spent the night at the Crown and Mitre in 1797 on the eve of his wedding in Carlisle Cathedral to a local Cumbrian girl, Margaret Carpenter.

In 1902 the old coaching inn was totally rebuilt, with no expense spared, four stories high in sandstone and red bricks and little towers at the top. The president of the USA, Woodrow Wilson stayed there on a state visit to the UK in 1918, insisting on stopping off in Carlisle as that had been the hometown of his mother, calling it a 'pilgrimage of the heart'.

By the 1950s, the hotel still had its Edwardian grandeur, with sweeping staircases and oak-panelled bars and dining rooms, head waiters in coat-tails, liveried doormen and the Crown and Mitre insignia picked out everywhere in gold, almost as if it were a royal residence. The ballroom was large and splendid and attracted the quality from the city and county who turned up for balls in their best and most formal evening wear. Not the sort of place that Ivy or any of her friends from the factory would ever frequent – though naturally very popular with Carr's directors. But it was known and admired, if just from the outside, a grand and dominating building right in the heart of the old city.

All day long, during the post-war years when Ivy was growing up, factory hooters constantly signalled the end of another shift. If you made the mistake of trying to get across the town at the wrong time, you would be swept along by thousands of workers released from their factories, flooding on to the street.

There was work for all, now that the factories were tooling up, hoping for a post-war boom, going back to peacetime production, back to the products they had always made. During the war, many had gone over to war work, making uniforms or rations for the troops.

In 1948, aged fifteen, Ivy, along with two other friends from school, decided to apply to Carr's, to join the girls she had shouted at from the playground. It was looked upon as a good job for girls of Ivy's class and education. She never saw 'cracker packer' as a term of contempt, unlike some of the more aspirational and middle-class Carlisle families. She saw smart girls, in smart overalls, who seemed to be cheerful and happy. Just like herself.

Everyone in Carlisle knew about Carr's. Its factory had dominated the skyline and the history of the city for so long – though most of its residents had probably forgotten its origins, or indeed how remarkable it was that a small city like Carlisle should have been the birthplace of biscuits as we know them today.

The story of Carr's began in 1831 when young Jonathan Dodgson Carr, the son of a grocer, opened his first bread shop in Castle Street in the middle of Carlisle, having walked there all the way from Kendal, about fifty miles south of the city. Kendal was in West-morland at the time, and Carlisle was in Cumberland

– both since 1974 neatly if not quite happily joined together in the new county of Cumbria.

However, 'walking all the way' is a bit of a Carr family legend. It is more than likely he got a lift most of the way from a family friend who was in the tea business, but it is true that, as a second son, he did set off alone, with a pack on his back, to seek his fortune

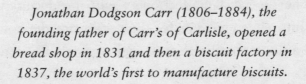

Jonathan Dodgson Carr (1806–1884), the founding father of Carr's of Carlisle, opened a bread shop in 1831 and then a biscuit factory in 1837, the world's first to manufacture biscuits.

in Carlisle, which, although with a population of just 30,000, was a bigger town than Kendal with more opportunities, where industry appeared to be booming and the railways rumoured to be coming soon.

When Jonathan Dodgson Carr opened his little bread shop, biscuits were not as we know them today. The word biscuit was in use, but it generally referred to ship's biscuits. In Dr Johnson's famous dictionary in 1775, he gave two definitions for biscuits. Firstly he said they were, 'a kind of hard dry biscuit, made to be carried at sea'. Ship's biscuits were made from hard-baked unleavened dough, which lasted much better on long voyages than bread. A seaman would tap the biscuit on a hard surface before eating it in order to dislodge the weevils. Ship's biscuits were usually made in ports, all by hand, in a bakery near the docks, then transferred to the boats when they set off on a long voyage. When Captain Cook did his epic voyages across the globe in the 1770s, he managed to make some of his hard tack biscuits last for up to three years.

There were also sweet biscuits, commonly known as 'fancies'. Dr Johnson defined them as 'compositions of fine flour, almonds, sugar, made by confectioners'.

The specialist confectioners who produced sweet biscuits tended to cater for the quality, for the nobility and affluent middle classes, and were usually centred in the wealthy areas, such as Mayfair in London.

In the eighteenth and early nineteenth centuries, these sweet biscuits were not taken with tea or coffee, as today, but were considered by the upper classes as an important part of the dessert course. You dipped your biscuits in sweet wine to round off your meal. The most popular were sponge biscuits, often long and thin, made specially to fit into the narrow wine glasses of the time. (Sponge fingers today are often long and thin, reflecting their history.)

Sweet biscuits often came in fancy shapes, decorated with elaborate motifs, such as the Prince of Wales feather, or with some other royal connection. In most big towns, high-class confectioners made their own biscuits and supplied them to the wealthy. Some of the more successful published their own recipe books, with instructions on making your own biscuits at home. Sweet biscuits were also made by housewives in their homes, who might sell some of their spares from trays on the streets.

All these early biscuits, either hard tack or fancy sweet biscuits, were handmade, local productions by local bakers. No powered machinery was used. The sweet biscuits could not be transported more than a few miles, and even then it would need a fast stage-coach or they would very quickly go off. They certainly could not be sent off across the ocean to the far corners of the world.

All this changed, thanks to Jonathan Dodgson Carr. Having made a success of his bakery in Castle Street, he decided in 1837 to open his own biscuit-making factory.

This was the same factory that young Ivy, aged fifteen, applied to for a job in the autumn of 1948, 111 years later.

Chapter 2
Ivy

Ivy had to have a medical when she applied to Carr's, as did all new factory workers all over the country. She was frightened by the thought of possibly having to strip and be examined by a doctor, but in the event all they seemed concerned about was her nails.

'You were not allowed nail varnish and you hadn't to have bitten your nails. One of the girls I applied with was turned because of the state of her nails, but I got accepted. I was then told to go and pick up my overalls.

'I went home and wore them all evening, in fact, I never had them off for that first week. I wanted everyone in the street to see me, show them I was in work.

'Anyway, the next day, wearing my overalls, I arrived early for my first day, as I was so eager to start work. I stood looking through the windows. I could see all the girls working away. I remember thinking – I can't imagine what it will be like, what will I do? I just had no expectations. And of course I never thought for one moment that I would end up working there for so many years.'

At the end of that first day, Ivy and another girl decided to go home along the canal.

'As we were walking along, just the two of us, this man suddenly flashed himself. What a fright we got. We ran like hell and caught up with a group of other Carr's workers, walking from the factory. We felt safer then.

'At the time, I was really scared, as it had never happened before, and I had never seen such a thing. I suppose what I should have done, which I might have done today, was go up to him and start singing "Oh what a beauty".

'Don't you know that song? Could be an old music hall song. I learned it when I was young. No, not from my mother, she would never have sung a song like that. It might have been on the Billy Cotton Band show, just after the war.

> *Oh what a beauty,*
> *Never seen one like that before*
> *Oh what a beauty*
> *It must be two feet long or more*
> *It's such a lovely colour*
> *Nice and round and fat*
> *I never thought a marrow*
> *Could grow as big as that*

'That would have fettled him! I would have laughed in his face right enough. But I was only fifteen at the time, and too scared. So I ran home.'

*

Jonathan Dodgson Carr would have been appalled by such behaviour, as well as by the rude song that Ivy so enjoyed singing. He was a Quaker and when he opened his new biscuit works in 1837, he was determined that all his workers should be of good moral character and behaviour.

He had chosen for his new factory a site in Caldewgate, just outside the old walled city. It was a poor area, with many slums, situated beside the river and a canal, down which ships sailed for the open sea.

He had done his research and experimenting and his new factory turned out to be revolutionary – the first in the world to make biscuits on an industrial scale, using steam-powered machinery and production lines. He created a machine for cutting biscuits, which until then had been cut by hand, taking the idea from a printing machine that he had seen in use at the tin factory of his friend Hudson Scott. He also adapted the system of cutting out letters, as done in the printing works, when it came to the shapes of his biscuits. One of Carr's first lines of biscuits were alphabet biscuits, greatly loved by generations of Victorian children. It was later considered to be one of the important tools in helping the Victorians to read.

Hudson Scott, like Jonathan Dodgson Carr, was a Quaker. It is often said that those early nineteenth-century Quaker families, who did so much to create and finance the industrial revolution, were part of a Quaker mafia. It is remarkable how many there were at the same time creating remarkable institutions – the Cadburys, Rowntrees and Frys in chocolates and sweets, the Lloyds and Barclays in banking, Clarks in shoes, Wedgwood in pottery. Behind the scenes were other Quakers, like the Pease family who helped finance the first railway lines. And yet at the time the Quakers were only a small minority of the British population, rarely more than 100,000. (Today they are greatly reduced, numbering only 14,000 adult members.)

They did tend to know each other, which helped with contacts, but they did not do discounts or favours for each other. They usually ended up being deadly rivals, which is eventually what happened in the biscuit trade.

But the big thing about them was that they were trusted, their word was their bond, no need for contracts or legal agreements, which their fellow Quakers knew as well as the general public. They might be dour, sombrely dressed, refusing to take oaths or accept any hierarchies, thus cutting themselves off from so many professions, such as the law, the army, academia, but they were incredibly hard-working, honest, inventive and entrepreneurial.

They had at one time been victimised for their non-conformist beliefs, and disliked by many ordinary folks for their moralising, sanctimonious ways and rules, such as their insistence that all their workers should be abstemious – in every way.

An indenture dated 1849, signed by a new apprentice baker at the Carr's factory, John Sanderson of Ashley Street, Carlisle – site of Ivy's school – shows that he had to agree 'not to commit fornication nor contract matrimony, nor play at Cards or Dice tables. He shall neither buy nor sell. He shall not haunt Taverns or Playhouses nor absent himself from his Master's service day or night unlawfully.' And he had to keep this up for the whole five years of his apprenticeship.

On the other hand, Carr's paid good wages, provided reading rooms, a large wash bath big enough to swim in, medical and educational help, none of which his workers had at home. Jonathan Dodgson Carr created model terrace houses for his workers – naming the first street Kendal Street, after the town where he had been born.

A report in *Chambers Edinburgh Journal* of 9 September 1848 praises the running of the Carr's factory and the good health of the workers, comparing it favourably with London bakers, who had been investigated in a previous edition of the *Journal* and found to be over-worked, undernourished and badly treated. In contrast, Carr's workers were well dressed and of a 'healthy appearance'. But then, they were allowed very few unhealthy habits.

Jonathan Dodgson Carr had chosen the Caldewgate site partly because it was on the canal – the one along which Ivy had walked on her first day. It had been built in 1823, just eleven miles to the sea, but it gave him shipping access down to Liverpool and to the wider world, for importing raw materials and for dispatching his biscuits, which until then, like all biscuits, had enjoyed only local circulation. By the 1840s he was already sending his biscuits to London.

And at the time he was building his new factory he also knew that the railways were coming. For some time canals had been established all over the country with great success, but the Carlisle to Port Carlisle canal arrived late – and alas was killed off by the noisy newcomer before it had properly flourished. It was later filled in and converted into a railway line.

The world's first railway was George Stephenson's Stockton to Darlington in 1825 – backed by the local Quakers – followed by the first passenger line, the Liverpool–Manchester in 1830. There were then plans for a cross-country line, from Newcastle to Carlisle, which eventually arrived in 1836, just before the Carr's factory opened. Carr's then created their own branch line, with a terminus inside their factory boundary.

In the very early years of the factory, there seems to have been only two sorts of biscuits produced – the alphabet biscuits and a form of dry water biscuits. By the end of the 1840s, the factory was producing up to twenty different types. A diary kept by a foreman, John Irving, for the year 1849 records him being made foreman of 'the Sugar Biscuit and Ginger Cake Department'. He describes new machines coming in to make Excursion biscuits – which would appear to have been made specially for the annual works outing – and another machine to make Pic-Nic biscuits, named after the fashionable pasttime of having picnics in parks.

His diary entry for 4 February 1851 reads 'Got a blowing up from John Carr about the ginger nuts being too hard baked', and on 12 June he writes 'Got little finger of the right hand broken with the Dessert Machine'.

The name Rich Dessert biscuits harked back to those aristocratic diners dunking their sweet biscuits in their glass of sweet wine. There was also Captain's Thin, a dry biscuit, a reference to the sort of better quality hard tack which the captain of the ship might have treated himself to.

Following up on the success of the Alphabet biscuits, there were a couple of other fun lines, which did very well with families. Doggie biscuits were not for dogs but carried illustrations of the best-known and best-loved dogs and were officially known as the Kennel Range. They featured Labradors, terriers and greyhounds. Children and dog lovers enjoyed collecting and eating them, but the problem was that their prominent features, such as their nose or ears or tails, tended to get broken off. Customers complained, hoping to get a new biscuit in return, till eventually the line was withdrawn.

Another popular line caused far less trouble as the image was flat, with no sticky-out bits. They carried the engravings of well-known and distinguished people of the time, such as Queen Victoria, the Duke of Wellington and the Prince of Wales, plus all-time greats like Shakespeare. The images were not all that clear, which was part of the fun, trying to work out who on earth they were.

By the 1840, Carr's biscuits had been reaching London, and in a good condition, thanks not only to the rail and sea transport, but also to the good packaging, which was due to the dexterity of the biscuit packers. No such form of labour had been needed when all biscuits were handmade and went straight from the baker's back oven on to the counter at the front of the shop. A new breed of working life had been created.

In 1841, Jonathan Dodgson Carr suddenly achieved some national acclaim. In some senses it was a minor award as it did not come with any prize money, but it was remarkable in that it gave recognition to a biscuit factory that had been going only a few years, situated in a town a long way from anywhere, created by a family with no connections to the good and the great of the time, and in a field that had quickly become crowded, with biscuit factories beginning to spring up all over the country, from Edinburgh to Reading, once J.D. had shown the way. Carr's was honoured with a Royal Warrant for biscuits – the first biscuit manufacturer to receive this royal seal of approval.

No one seems to know how it happened, whether some lobbying had gone on, friends in high places had been tapped up, or a generous supply of free samples had been slipped into the royal kitchens – not, of course, that Quakers would stoop to such tricks.

It does seem to have come out of the blue. What seems likely is that the royal household must genuinely have sampled and enjoyed some of Carr's biscuits – which particular ones were never revealed – but once it happened, Jonathan Dodgson made the most of it. He referred to the Royal Warrant in their promotion and advertising, knowing how much it would make his rivals jealous and furious, but of course it was done discreetly, without too much shouting.

One of the company's earlier advertisements appeared in *The Friend*, the journal of the Quakers, in 1845. 'The Queen's biscuits manufactured by J.D. Carr, Carlisle, are in general use at the Royal Household and much approved by numerous respectable families.'

Naturally, the packaging of the biscuits was soon emblazoned with the royal coats of arms and the proud wording: 'By Appointment to the Her Majesty, Queen Victoria, Biscuit Manufacturers, Carr and Co, Carlisle, Established AD 1831'.

Those words and the impressive logo were still being used by the time Ivy joined the firm in 1948, though now His Majesty had to be thanked, as there was a king on the throne, George VI.

As a factory-line worker, Ivy found herself handling packets all emblazoned with the Royal Warrant, just as her predecessors on the line had done for over the previous hundred years.

The factory which fifteen-year-old Ivy entered was still owned and run by the Carr family, but few of them had remained Quakers. Fortunately for all their new young healthy, eager post-war workers, the insistence on chastity and temperance had ceased to be applied. No contract had to be signed promising not to commit fornication or visit playhouses or play dice.

However, the company still tried to be benevolent, carrying on the family tradition of treating the workers well, more or less, depending on the new post-war economic and social times. And young women like Ivy were pleased, nay quite proud, to be employed at Carr's factory, the 'Home of Biscuits', as it proclaimed outside on the factory wall.

Ivy did not keep a diary or any account of her first year working at Carr's, and has to rely on her memory to recall exactly what she did, what she wore, what the factory was like in 1948 – but by chance there is an account of a visit to the factory that very same year by a young schoolgirl. She was on a school visit to the factory, which many local schools enjoyed at the time and for many decades afterwards, though it has largely died out, thanks to that modern practice of health and safety and also the unwillingness of factories in these straitened times to devote staff to acting as guides.

The age of the schoolgirl is not known, but it would appear she was probably around fifteen, nor is her name, but she was a pupil at Dalston, a village five miles to the south of Carlisle. Presumably the teacher asked all the pupils to write an account of their visit – and this one was sent to Carr's and appeared in the factory magazine.

MY VISIT TO CARR'S

On Monday, the 22nd March 1948, we, the scholars from Dalston National School, went to Carlisle on the 1.45 p.m. bus to Carr's biscuit works.

On arriving at the works we were a little early, so we were ushered into the café to await the arrival of one of the directors and the guides. The corridor and the café were both panelled in lovely oak wood and the wooden block floors were highly polished. The room itself had big windows which made the room very light, and the beautiful pictures which hung on the wall were lovely country scenes painted in exquisite colours.

About 2.30 p.m. one of the executives, a Mr Sarginson, came in and gave us a description of the origin of the firm. He said that the works, which were over a hundred years old, were founded by J.D. Carr in 1831. He first started with a small bakery business in Castle Street; the business grew and so he had to find larger premises. In 1834 he invented the first machine in the whole world to stamp out biscuits. In the year 1841 he was granted a Royal Appointment to Queen Victoria. Then he went on to say that Carr's exported to nearly every country in the world, and they had all sort of trades like engineers, printers, joiners and electricians.

We were divided into groups of six each under a separate guide. Our guide, Miss Tomlinson, explained everything wonderfully and she told us everything.

First, we went across the yard into the room where all the ingredients were mixed up into a dough. Next we entered the room where the biscuits were cooked. The ovens were 160 feet long and were really marvellous modern ovens. We stood quite a while watching two women making oatcakes. We were really fascinated by their efficiency, expertness and quickness of hand. The rooms were not sombre, dark, and miserable. They were light, cool and a happy atmosphere hung in the air wherever we went.

Upstairs where the girls packed the tins for export the tins were all covered over in brightly coloured labels of all kinds. The making of the chocolate biscuits was really very interesting, the way they mixed all the ingredients together into a stiff paste. When we had been in that room we went into the room where the biscuits were put on the chocolate and another layer of chocolate on top. As the biscuits came through, a girl who sat on one side of the machine separated the biscuits with a needle so they wouldn't stick together.

Some of the export biscuits were carefully packed in tins with shavings down each side to keep them firm. Then they were passed on to another girl who soldered round the top and marked her number on the side. After this they were taken to another two girls who dipped them in a large tank full of water to see if they were airtight, and if they weren't they were passed back to the girl.

Journeying on we came to the print room where girls fed machines which printed magazines and all kinds of labels. We then went to see the guillotine, a machine which a man operated by *pressing down a lever which brought the guillotine down, and so cut through the paper, and just as he pressed the lever a guard flew out to keep him off it.*

The process I thought most interesting was the first one where the ingredients were all mixed together into a stiff dough, rolled out into sheets, and put on to a machine, and as it passed through each roller the dough got thinner and thinner until just the right thickness. Then it went through a machine which stamped out the shape of the biscuit. It was then cut to the shape and the waste went below and back to the beginning while the biscuits moved on into the vast ovens.

Passing through the rooms with the ovens we looked through one of the little doors, and gas jets were at the top and bottom to bake both the top and underneath of the biscuits.

From here we came to another room where the now lovely cooked golden brown, rich appetising biscuits waited to be packed by the girls.

I wouldn't mind working in the offices as I would like to do general office work, but I wouldn't like to work in the factory as I don't think I would be quick enough.

The account is well written, well punctuated, a tribute, some might suggest, to the post-war education system.

At the end, the magazine editor says that he has printed it exactly as she wrote it, but says she made one mistake. The date of the first cutting machine was 1849, so he says, not 1834. It could of course not have been 1834 as the factory did not open till 1839, but it is more likely to have been 1839 than 1849. In fact this date has never been properly agreed upon.

The girl describes some of the jobs which Ivy herself had to do at that time, such as stuffing paper shavings into tins as packaging. The schoolgirl also describes activities which Ivy never mentions, or perhaps was unaware of, such as girls soldering tins and dipping them into water to make sure they were airtight. Also, separating biscuits with a needle. Could she have got that right? Sounds very primitive for what was supposed to be an up-to-date factory.

She also graphically describes the biscuits being stamped out, a process created over a hundred years earlier by Jonathan Dodgson Carr.

On their tour, the girls clearly received a bit of company PR, given some of the stirring history of the firm, but the schoolgirl reporter ends by saying that while she would like a job at Carr's, she would like to be in the office, not on the production line. She carefully does not suggest this is because she must have seen how hard, how tedious, how back-breaking packing biscuits could be for women like Ivy, but nicely turns it against herself, saying she would not be 'quick enough'.

Chapter 3
Ivy

When Ivy started at Carr's in 1948 the works were very much as the Dalston schoolgirl had described – except she went first into the office block, noticing the lovely oak wood and the wooden block floors. The ordinary workers, like Ivy, never had occasion to go into the posh, impressive office area.

The main entrance, which had a clock tower, was through an arch beside what had once been an old granary. In the entry yard was an ornamental fishpond, stocked with fish. The office workers went left into the office block while the workers processed down a long, rather prison-like concrete corridor leading to the factory buildings, where the biscuits were mixed and made and baked.

There were lots of little separate buildings for the various processes, such as the chocolate room, the cream room, the custard cream room, now morphed together into one large factory area, with the corridor now much longer than it used to be, joining up the various areas. The object now is to keep all those involved in food processing under one roof and today this long and bleak green-painted concrete corridor is known by the workers as the Green Mile – a nickname taken from the Hollywood film based on the novel by Stephen King – which is about death row.

In the forties and fifties, the corridor was not as long, but still fairly intimidating and scary for a young girl, though the business of washing hands and tying up hair was not as intensive as it is today. And when Ivy started, individual lockers had not come in, as workers took their own uniforms home.

The plant itself covered over seventeen acres, with many different buildings and departments, yards and alleyways, all very confusing for new workers. Apart from the office block, the main buildings included the boiler house, the training centre, the engineers' department, plus the different biscuit-, chocolate- and cream-making areas. The sickly sweet aroma of the biscuits, which could be smelled out in the streets of Caldewgate, and in the playground of Ivy's old school, became more intense as you walked down the long corridor. The strongest smells in the forties and fifties were of chocolate. Water biscuits, by comparison, have little smell, even in the heart of the baking and packaging process.

When Ivy started, the old canal that led to the sea had long been filled in, but the canal basin could still clearly be seen and workers walked along it, as Ivy had done. The little railway siding connected to the main line especially for Carr's was coming to the end of its life, but Ivy can remember one old engine when she first started – which was in fact still in operation until the 1960s. It was a fireless steam engine, the water heated up from the factory boilers, which could run for a few hours at a time in the yard, shunting wagons.

'I have a memory of the engine getting out of control one day, bursting out of the yard and into the street, terrifying everyone in Caldewgate. It must have been a queer sight. I never saw that happening, at least I don't think I did. I think someone told me. It was a long time ago.' (She had probably been told about a well-known incident from the 1920s, photographs of which still exist, when some railway wagons did run out of the yard and into Caldewgate.)

There was constant noise, not just from the machinery but from large lorries going in and out all day, delivering raw materials and taking away the finished biscuits.

The whole, sprawling factory had an institutional feel, like a Victorian school, with all the brick buildings, but of course much bigger than any school that Ivy or any other Carlisle girl had ever experienced. When Ivy first started, there were around 2,500 to 3,000 people working in the factory. All pretty frightening and confusing for any young girl starting out in her adult working life.

'It all seemed so big and daunting. I was very nervous, worried about speaking to anyone, or doing the wrong things. I never answered back to anyone who might tell me off. I did what I was told, which was to stay on my line and not leave it.'

Ivy's first job was on the Tuppenny Packets, a simple, obvious, basic sort of job most girl beginners started on in the 1940s which was relatively easy to learn and hard to do much damage, either to yourself or the precious biscuits. The rate for a fifteen-year-old girl at the time was thirty-four shillings (£1.60p) a week – as detailed in an official weekly rate sheet issued by the factory on 14 November 1947. There was an agreed bonus rate that could get you up to thirty-four shillings if you achieved your piecework rates, depending on how many pieces of work you completed in a set time. At the age of sixteen, it jumped to forty-one shillings while the top basic rate, for a woman of twenty-one years of age zoomed up to sixty-five shillings.

'All I had to do was put four shortcake biscuits or four ginger nuts, or whatever it was that day, and put them in a packet, fold the ends and seal it. It then went on for someone else to do the netting, which was what we called putting the labels on. You had to be quick, mind, and keep up the work rate, to earn your bonus.'

Her uniform consisted of her long white overall, buttoned down the front, reaching almost to the knees.

She was given two sets for which she was responsible, having to wash and repair them herself. A charge hand, the next grade up, wore a pink overall; a forewoman wore a blue overall while a supervisor, the top position for an ordinary worker, as opposed to management or office staff, wore blue and white overalls. The uniform varied over the years, and the job titles, but it meant it was easy to see the bosses hovering from a long distance away.

'We were also issued with a white cap and told that our hair had to be tucked under our cap. No hair at all had to be showing. If you had quite long hair, you had to pull your cap right down. Some of them looked queer and funny. There was one girl wore her cap right down and she looked as if she was in a cowboy film, you know, sitting on the wagon trail.'

The brim of the cap was stiff and Ivy's mother used to starch it for her, to keep its shape. Ivy was insistent her overall had to be washed each week and complained if it was not getting clean enough, even when it was done at her grandmother's wash house with its ace boiler. Sometimes her mother would spare no expense and send it to the Lakeland Laundry.

After a week or so on Tuppenny Packets, Ivy was moved to lining tins – putting greaseproof paper inside empty tins, which would then be filled by other girls. Then she had a spell putting paper shavings in the tins, padding to protect the biscuits on their long sea journey to the ends of the known world. There was none of the sort of stuff used to protect fragile goods today, no inflated plastic bags or polystyrene pellets. For a while she was on netting, given a pile of labels and a pot of glue, sticking them on packets or tins as they processed past.

During her first year, she was moved round quite frequently on to different production lines, but always basically doing the same – packing biscuits and crackers, most of it done by hand.

When Ivy moved on to slightly messier jobs, involving liquid cream or chocolate, she took to wearing what she called a belly band – a piece of material which she tied round her middle and fixed with tape, so that any grease or liquid chocolate or hot cream or other sticky runny sweet stuff did not ruin the front of her precious overalls.

She worked surrounded in the various packing rooms by between ten and thirty other girls or young women. The only men around were the barrowmen, who came in at regular intervals to wheel away the filled tins, some of which were enormous, holding about ten pounds of biscuits.

She didn't find it boring or even monotonous. Some rooms could be very noisy, if they were near heavy machinery, or very hot if they were near the ovens, but Ivy was mostly spared such places. Girls were not supposed to move from their station, unless told.

She joined the union as soon as she arrived at Carr's but can't remember what it was called. 'I just did it because of my mother. The moment I started she said, "Now, don't forget to join the union, Ivy." Everyone did in them days.'

While doing her work a lot of her time was spent talking, laughing and singing with the other girls, though not of course when a charge hand or supervisor was around. 'You were meant to concentrate on the job in hand, not muck around or enjoy yourself.

'You were also meant not to walk around, but stay in your department. When I came into work each day, I used to love looking at the fishpond. I got it into my head that one of the fish, a very white fish, was called Ivy, and it had been named after me. I used to tell all the other girls that – and they believed it.'

The girls didn't swear back in the 1940s, according to Ivy, at least she only heard the F-word once: 'It was a girl called Daisy – and she was off the fairgrounds. She came out with the F-word one day and I said to her what my mother used to say. "A decent man wouldn't swear in front of a lady, let alone a lady in front of another lady."'

One of the features of the pre-war years at Carr's, which had started back in the very early years of the factory, was a works outing. Quakers, though they were tough on slackers and those with loose morals and laid down very strict working conditions, were always keen for their workers to enjoy some sort of communal fun day, usually a grand outing.

Another Quaker firm and one of Carr's major competitors was Huntley & Palmers of Reading. They had their annual do in the factory itself, tastefully decorating it with flowers and plants, then sitting everyone down at long wooden tables for a good tuck-in. Husbands and wives were invited, plus guests. These factory suppers, usually held in April, finished with some sort of entertainment, such as a magic lantern show.

At Carr's, they always had proper outings, for the whole factory, which J.D. first started in 1840, at which time the workforce was still quite small and manageable. They became so famous in Carlisle that workers elsewhere were resentful that they did not have such treats.

The 1850 outing, with the whole factory being closed for the day, started at 4.30 in the morning when the entire workforce, which by then numbered 111, plus husbands, wives and children, plus all the Carr family, including J.D., his wife and six children and other relatives, gathered at Carlisle railway station, with the younger children wildly excited at the thought of their first train ride. They steamed off to Cockermouth thirty-seven miles away, where ten large horse-drawn coaches were waiting to take them to Derwentwater where they had breakfast in the grounds of a hotel, hampers having been unloaded and the food laid out on tables in the garden. The bread, baked by a volunteer staff the night before, was still warm. It was eaten with ham and cheese and plenty of boiled eggs. No alcohol was allowed with any of the meals that day.

They then split into different parties, doing different activities, from climbing Skiddaw to sailing on Derwentwater, plus games, entertainments, and lots more eating and drinking, tea and lemonade being provided all day. It was almost midnight before they all rolled back into Carlisle railway station. Next day, not one person

Carr's workers in their best frocks eating sandwiches
on their annual outing in the 1930s

was late for work. The whole outing had cost J.D. £40
– which he knew was worth it ten times over in the
pleasure it had given and the goodwill it generated.

Later Carr's works outings went to the seaside, such
as Silloth, the local seaside resort on the Solway, loved
by generations of Carlisle people, and also to Blackpool. There were even occasions in the 1920s and
1930s when the Carr's works outings reached Paris
and Brussels – all paid for by the company.

Alas for Ivy and her post-war co-workers, still struggling under rationing and other restrictions, the big
outing, for the whole works, with the factory closed
for the day and entertainment and refreshments laid
on, seems to have died out by 1948.

'The only outing I can remember was one organised by the bakehouse. A group of us went on the train
to Blackpool. I remember two girls saying they didn't
want to sit next to so and so – who was a charge hand.
I think we organised the outing ourselves, not the
factory. And I think we paid for it.'

For well over a hundred years, Blackpool had been
the number one attraction for all northern families,
including Scottish families, who came in their tens of
thousands during their Fair Week or holiday week,
jamming the streets of Carlisle as they headed for Blackpool in their coaches. The main route south was through
the town centre, until the M6 motorway was completed
in the 1970s and Carlisle could breathe more freely.

Blackpool was seen as glamorous, exciting, with so much to do and see, such as the tower (built 1894), the pleasure beach, all the big shows at the big theatres, and the annual illuminations. They began on a small scale in 1879 when eight so-called 'electric sunshine' arc lights were hung on the promenade, but became world famous from 1912 onwards when Princess Louise turned on 10,000 lights and the illuminations proper began. By the 1950s, when Ivy visited, there were one million light bulbs and seventeen million annual visitors. Numbers fell by the sixties, when cheap foreign travel arrived, but it is still the UK's number one seaside tourist.

Carlisle families, who could afford it, took their annual holidays in Blackpool in the immediate post-war years, or went on day trips by coach on so called mystery tours which usually turned out to be a tour round the Lakes or joining the millions on the front at Blackpool. The men would have dragged several wooden crates of State Management beer on to the coach before departure, which they would open up on the way back, swigging the beer and singing songs, till soon the whole coach joined in, and they rolled back into Carlisle in the early hours.

Carlisle, however, also had its own well-loved little local seaside town – Silloth situated on the Solway, about ten miles from Carlisle. It has also had a long history as a seaside resort, if on a more modest scale, starting from the 1860s onwards, once the railway had opened. Silloth was not seen as glamorous and exciting like Blackpool, with all its facilities – the main adjective describing Silloth usually is 'bracing' – but it provided lots of harmless, healthy fun for generations of Carlisle families.

Everyone went there at some time in the summer, whole streets emptying as neighbourhoods went en masse, the overexcited children rushing up and down the platform at the Citadel station, then jamming into overcrowded carriages, dying for their first glimpse of the sea.

Silloth's handsome main street was filled with hotels, boarding houses, cafes and shops, overlooking an enormous green, beautifully kept and cut. Beyond it was the promenade and the sea, with great views across the Solway to Criffel and the Scottish hills. Most people walked up and down the promenade and paddled in the sea, though there wasn't much sand in Silloth itself. You had to go down the coast a bit, to West Silloth, for that, where there was a golf course and a residential home.

Entertainment in the pre-war and immediate post-war years included a Pierrot show, fun fair, donkey rides and an amusement arcade. There was also a dock and little harbour to poke around at Silloth, with cargo boats coming in from Glasgow and Liverpool, some of them bringing wheat for Carr's flour mill by the dock side. There was also a little fishing fleet, bringing in Solway shrimps, which you could buy fresh in the town. The basic population of 3,000 would swell to 10,000 in the summer season during the fifties. When the railway station closed in 1964, Silloth's great days were over, but it is still enormously loved and lingers on in the minds and affections of all Carlisle people.

All the Carr's biscuit workers, Ivy included were taken there as children and as young adults went off there with their pals for their Saturday afternoons or Sundays off work to have a bit of a blow, parade up and down, before going back to the grind on Monday.

'When I was younger, going to Silloth seemed to be going a million miles away. I went on the train with my parents and grandmother and my brother. I could never sleep the night before if I knew we were going. I was just so excited.

'But going to Blackpool on that works trip was a really big adventure. I had never been as far on the train. We just seemed to laugh all the time. I have a photo somewhere of us all at the railway station, lining up before we set off. I think it must have been around 1953. Now I look at it, there are far more than I remember – looks about a hundred. Yet it was just the bakehouse workers.'

Ivy never drank, never went to pubs, even as a young working woman. 'My father liked a pint and would go to the Horse and Farrier in Raffles on a Saturday evening, but he never drank in the house. No one drank at home, in their own house. Now it's what everyone does.'

She went on a mystery tour once, not long after she had started at Carr's, with another girl from her production line. The mystery tour destination turned out to be the Lakes, so not much of a mystery. When they landed in Keswick they were told there was a one-hour stop for shopping or walking around, or going down to the lake.

'Me and my friend decided to go to a pub. I had never been to one before. I went in – and oh no, sitting there was one of our neighbours. I was so embarrassed. I worried all the way home to Carlisle, knowing my mother would be bound to find out. So when I got home, I told her. I thought it was better coming from me than from a neighbour. Young women never went to pubs. It just wasn't done.'

Now and again, being nosy, when there were no charge hands glaring over her, young Ivy wandered round the factory. It was a bit of a rabbit warren, with much of it still as it was when J.D. had first built it. One day down an alleyway she came across two women tearing up paper – teasing it out to make packing material for the boxes of biscuits.

'They had built up a huge mountain of torn paper, as big as a haystack. I decided to climb up and started jumping on this mountain of paper, imagining I was on a farm in a hayloft. From down below I heard one of the girls shouting up to me, "Here's Polly!" This was Polly Parker, the supervisor. We were all really scared of her. I jumped down from the pile of paper and hid behind some tins, saying to myself, "Please God, don't let her look up here." But she just walked through our room, and never noticed I was missing.

'It was just devilment, really, being young and daft. I wasn't really naughty or wicked or anything. I was just enjoying myself. I always loved working there, from day one.'

Ivy got a tea break each morning of ten minutes. Depending on what sort of job they were on, the girls would go singly or together. If it was a rush order, they would take it in turns, agreeing with the charge hand who would go and when. If times were slack, they would all take their break together in the canteen.

At lunch, when Ivy began in 1948, they were allowed one hour, but a few years later this was reduced to forty-five minutes. 'They even tried once to give us only thirty minutes for lunch, but we all protested. No strikes, we just moaned, and they stuck to the forty-five minutes.'

During the first week she was there, she went to the canteen for lunch, but didn't like it. 'I didn't know where to sit, so I just stood there, looking stupid, as all the girls seemed to be in groups. Someone said sit over there, with that woman. I did, but she turned out to have a funny eye. It upset me, which I know it shouldn't have done, so I never went back.'

Instead, Ivy decided she would go home for lunch each day as Dalton Avenue was only a mile or so away. She went on the bus at first, but it became expensive and was all a bit of rush, so she bought herself a bike. Her first one was a Hercules, bought from T.P. Bell in Abbey Street where generations of Carlisle teenagers got their bikes. She bought it on the never-never, paying five shillings a week.

'I loved my bike and was never off it. You felt so free, whizzing along on your bike, independent like. I used to cycle so hard there and back every lunch time that when I got off my bike my little legs were shaking.'

She received her wages every week on a Thursday, lining up to retrieve it from a little black metal box with her personal number on. 'It was a very small box – cos our wages were so small!'

She handed over all her thirty-four shillings wages to her mother each week, who then gave her five shillings back as her pocket money, and another five shillings went on payments on her bike.

'I was always a homebody, and I loved coming home for my dinner. In fact, I never wanted to leave home, ever. I felt safe there.'

In her early working years, while still a teenager, she went with her mother and father each week to the cinema, as she had done while at school. During the war and the post-war years, every cinema in Carlisle, as in every town in the country, had massive queues, often winding round the block and stretching for several streets. These queues were despite the fact that in these post-war years Carlisle had as many as eight cinemas in operation. The Lonsdale, the smartest and biggest, had opened in 1931, but there were also several much older ones: the Palace (1906), the Public Hall (1907), the City (1915) as well as the Botchergate, Stanley, Rex, Regal, all of them going full steam, with queues for every film, whatever it was.

There was also a theatre, Her Majesty's, with live shows, which first opened in 1880. Charlie Chaplin and Buffalo Bill had appeared there in 1904. Many well-known music hall stars still performed there when Ivy was growing up, if not all of them perhaps quite at their peak. Seasons of plays were also performed at Her Majesty's by visiting companies, plus amateur shows by local theatricals, along with Gilbert and Sullivan. Going out, 'up street', as they say in Carlisle, there was quite a choice of entertainment in the post-war years.

TV was very rare. There were only 14,500 TV sets in the whole of the country in 1948, mostly around London. Even if TV had reached Carlisle, it would have been hard to switch on – one quarter of houses still did not have electricity.

Radio was popular, with those who had electricity often connecting leads to their overhead light sockets – which meant you sat in the dark to listen, hoping there would not be an explosion. There were no pop music programmes or channels on the BBC – only on Radio Luxemburg, which arrived in 1948 and launched the first hit parade. No wonder cinema-going was at its peak in 1948 with such little competition. A third of the population went to the films at least once a week.

'My father loved the cinema but he had this thing about queuing, he hated doing it, so he would rush home from work and then all of us would run to the City cinema to catch the early house. My mother would have two pies ready for him, the minute he got inside the front door, and he would eat them as we rushed off to the City.

'They had this strange woman in the box office, who had long dark ringlets and wore a long red velvet old-fashioned dress. Nobody else in Carlisle dressed like her. Everyone was fascinated by her.

'We always went in the cheap seats, which meant you entered in a side door that took you right to the front rows. Often the show had started, so we crept in, blinking in the dark, like three blind mice. *The Three Stooges*, that was one I loved, and of course Charlie Chaplin.'

Ivy enjoyed dancing – and another near reprimand

at work happened when she was almost caught by a supervisor. She was dancing by herself, behind a row of large biscuit tins, when a supervisor was seen to be approaching, but Ivy managed to get to her packing position on the line, just in time.

Now and again, when she got a bit older, she would go with girlfriends into the dance halls in the middle of town. She would dress up to the nines, putting on her nylons. 'I wore them with a panty girdle, or was it a suspender belt? Something like that. You had to, to keep them up.'

She went dancing at the Cameo and Queens, though never the Crown and Mitre, Carlisle's grand hotel, which had its own ballroom with proper musicians in evening dress, the sort of hotel which ordinary factory workers did not patronise.

Mostly, in her early teenage years, Ivy went to the community hall weekly hops at Raffles, and most of the girls and the boys there would be ones she had grown up with.

'I wasn't really all that good at dancing, but I did enjoy the quickstep.

'When I first started going, my mother used to say, "Now mind yourself, Ivy, I want you home by nine o'clock." And of course I did what I was told, being a good obedient little girl, even though I was by then a working woman.

'Girls of that age today are like cats. They only go

out in the dark. Instead of coming home at nine, as I did, that is the time they start thinking about going out.'

Several boys did ask to take her home, and now and again she agreed, usually in the company of another girl, just in case.

But she did progress now and again to allowing a boy to take her home, on her own. 'That usually ended in some struggles.'

There were men at work when Ivy joined Carr's, but they were in the minority – around 20 per cent of the 2,500 workers. In the very beginning, when the factory first opened back in 1837, there were only a hundred or so workers in the first few years, most of whom would appear to have been men, though no exact records have survived.

Jonathan Dodgson Carr had been a baker, which was a male occupation, so he employed men in his new factory when he first opened, usually taking them on as apprentices. But once the production lines started rolling, and J.D. Carr had introduced all the latest steam-powered machinery, cared for by men, he found that women could do the job of packing and filling the tins more dexterously and quickly, and more cheaply than the men.

This was the case all over the UK in the new factories of the Industrial Revolution, in which Britain was the world leader, especially in areas like textiles, food, sweets and chocolate. Until these factories of mass production came along, women on the whole did not go out to work, because there were no jobs for them – apart, of course, from domestic service, the main source of income for millions of women over the centuries.

Up until the last war, women workers had to leave once they were married, and always earned less than men, which was still the case when Ivy started at Carr's, though in just a few years, it was possible for married women to be employed.

One of the young boys Ivy remembers working with was Eric Wallace, born in Carlisle in 1938, who joined Carr's in 1953, by which time Ivy was now aged twenty.

Eric was unusual for a Carr's worker, male or female, that he had gone to what was then a small, modest fee-paying Catholic school, Austin Friars.

'I let my parents down badly by deciding to leave at the age of fifteen.' So Eric said later in a 2001 interview for Carlisle's oral archives. 'I didn't fancy any sort of academic career and decided I wanted to work in a factory, so I applied to Carr's. My father worked there fifty years in the end – and got a gold watch when he retired.

'I started as a glorified labourer – and loved it. For the first few weeks I went to bed at nine at night, absolutely shattered, but then I got used to it and really settled in.

'Then I became a barrow boy. It was like a great adventure playground, the most wonderful place for a young teenager to be. There were lots of new buildings but also lots of old buildings, going back to when Carr's began in the 1830s, full of mysterious passages. I used to love it in winter in the darkness, arriving at 7.30 in the morning, pitch black, dark streets, with cellars, attics and secret corridors – places where you could go to smoke a Woodbine.

'Because I was a barrow boy, one of Ronnie Atkins boys, a team of maybe a dozen teenagers, we could go everywhere in the factory with our barrows, picking up full tins of biscuits or carrying ingredients and materials, and wheel them round about the factory all day long.

'We were all teenage boys and there were lots of teenage girls, many more than us, so we were always falling in love. We would flirt, fall in and out of love and – er, hmm – there were many liaisons. We had the most wonderful time.

'We would meet in certain parts of the factory and then, after work, we would go to the Rex in Denton Holme or the Regal cinema across from the Carr's factory. You could get double seats, like sofas. And it was always very dark. Yes, it was tremendously exciting.'

Eric was then moved from the barrows to be a general labourer, and ordered to demolish some local houses surrounding the factory. These had been put up by J.D. Carr to house the workers but had now become slums.

'We had to knock down Poets' Corner – which was what we called these fairly squalid streets. They had been named Wordsworth Street, Shakespeare Street, Byron Street and I think a Coleridge Street. There were still one or two people living there. We had to go in with no training, no hard hats, no protective clothing, just a team of twenty or so of us told to get in there and knock down everything. We immediately had these great fires going, tied ropes round walls and chimneys to pull them down. It was brilliant. I couldn't wait to get into work every morning.'

Ivy never went out with Eric – he was a few years younger – but she remembers all the flirting that used to go on. And the occasional secret affairs.

One woman, a married woman, told her husband she only got one week's holiday a year, which was a lie, as she got two. During her other week off, her husband continued to drive her to work, dropped her off at the front gate, then went off to his own work. She would then go through the factory, out of a back door – and off to spend the day with her boyfriend. Her husband picked her up as usual at the front gates after work, never knowing what she had really been doing all day long.

Ivy eventually did get a move, a promotion of a sort, although at first she kept it quiet from her mother.

'She always said to me, when I first told her I wanted

to get a job at Carr's, that it would be all right by her, as long as I didn't work in the bakehouse.

'For the first few years I was in the packing rooms, then one day I was told I was being moved to the bakehouse, which would mean a little bit more money. I didn't tell my mother – not till six weeks after I had started.

'The thing people had against the bakehouse was that it was very hot and very noisy. The huge ovens were on night and day so there was constant heat and smoke. Sometimes you couldn't see for the smoke. I used to think they were on fire, especially when the bakehouse men started putting more paper in the ovens. They said it was a way of dampening the flames, which I never understood.'

The bakehouse was also more dangerous than the packing rooms, for the trays and the biscuits had just come out of the ovens, so handling them had to be done carefully.

'You could get the tips of your fingers burned if you were not careful and they would bleed. But of course you hadn't to show any blood. Otherwise you might get sent home.

'It was always well over 27 degrees Celsius in the bakehouse. But they did give you a glass of lemonade. They said it was to cool down your blood. So that was nice.'

Not complaining, well, not too much, about conditions in the factory was typical of the times in the post-war years. Women felt fortunate to have a steady job and at Carr's they felt they were being reasonably looked after and relatively well paid.

It was also typical of the times and perhaps of Carlisle people generally to accept things and conditions, almost proud not be ambitious, pushy, wanting or demanding, just to accept what came, what happened, as Ivy frequently observes. This can sound defeatist, sad, perhaps pathetic, but that would give the wrong impression. Despite thinking that 'nothing can be done, this is how it is' you can still be cheerful and strong like Ivy, and opinionated, speaking out when necessary. You know you have a function, a place in the world, humble though it is, and you are grateful to have it, knowing your place in the great scheme of things.

The idea of wanting to change things, demanding your rights, was rarely apparent in women workers or male workers for that matter, not during the forties and fifties. It was partly an effect of the recent war, when the population, not just service personnel, had for so long obeyed orders, did what they were told, accepted rationing and restrictions, shortages and deprivations. Putting yourself first, as opposed to your country, that all came much later.

Chapter 4
Dulcie

Bubbly Dulcie in her twenties

Dulcie was born on 26 September 1939, in Currock, one of Carlisle's council estates. She hated her Christian name when growing up, and still does. It sounds a bit posh and theatrical, as if she might have been named after Dulcie Gray, a well-known, well-loved English actress and singer during the war years, who married Michael Denison. In fact, Dulcie was named after a well-loved actress of the pre-war years – but an amateur one local to Carlisle, Dulcie Graham-Bowman. This was a time when amateur actresses had a loyal following who attended all their shows. It was Dulcie's grandmother, who loved the theatre, who insisted on the new baby being called Dulcie.

Dulcie and her two younger sisters lived with their mother and grandmother. There was a father, but Dulcie has little memory of him. 'He was hardly around. There were issues, so I never seemed to see him – and eventually they separated.'

Also living with them was a woman Dulcie always knew as Nana. 'She was a single mother at a time when it was disgraceful to have a baby and not be married. I think she had it adopted, then came to live with us. I never knew her relationship with my mother.'

Dulcie's mother worked at Carr's icing biscuits. She did the afternoon shift, her mother looking after Dulcie and her sisters, till she came home from work. Thanks to working at Carr's, her mother was able to buy broken biscuits very cheaply. 'She would bring home five-pound tins and if they were all chocolate biscuits, everyone would rush, the whole street, they were like gold nuggets. My favourites were Sports biscuits. My mother never made biscuits or baked anything herself. She was too busy working. So it was wonderful when she brought any biscuits home from work. We also used to buy biscuits at Woolworths, selecting our own, and a big slab of cake.'

Dulcie was in the Brownies and Guides and played a lot of sport, including tennis and particularly netball, representing Carlisle Girls. She followed the latest pop music on Radio Luxembourg.

Dulcie's mother did all the cooking, which was always fresh, as far as Dulcie remembers. They had a Sunday roast, then cold meat the next day with the vegetables fried up. They also had liver and onions, pasties and peas, usually with rice pudding for afters.

'There was no convenience food in these days, not for a long time. I remember when fish fingers came in we ate them all the time. We thought they were wonderful, and so handy and easy to cook – and eat.

'We usually had a bottle of sherry in the house, which was meant to be for Christmas only, but it always seemed to be going down. At Christmas we also had ginger wine, which my grandmother made. I would leave a glass out for Santa with a mince pie – which I presume my grandma drank and ate.

'My grandma lived with us and when we were all out at work, she would have an old friend in during the afternoons. When my mother came home from work she would say, "they've been at the sherry again". When the two old women were sitting nattering, I suppose they used to go and get the sherry bottle out.'

Dulcie attended Upperby primary school where, so she says, she was very good and passed the Eleven Plus for the Margaret Sewell – Carlisle's second-tier secondary school, after the crème had been selected for the high school. Girls who were directed to the Margaret Sewell were still considered to have passed the Merit.

'My mother didn't want me to go, saying she would not be able to afford the uniform, and anyway she wanted me to be a cracker packer, like her. But I insisted, so I went to the Margaret Sewell. I did well in my first year – and then I discovered boys in the Creighton School next door. It was downhill from then on. I mean, downhill with my school work.'

She did manage to master a bit of typing, but was unable to get the hang of shorthand, which Margaret Sewell girls were taught in order to prepare them for office work.

So when Dulcie was fifteen her mother got her desire. Dulcie left school and went straight to Carr's. Her mother being there helped her to get an interview and be accepted. She has no memory of her nails or anything else being inspected, but then she had secured a rather unusual and attractive job, perhaps thanks to her mother's influence.

She was not put on a production line like her mother or like Ivy – after all, she had gone to the Maggie Ann, as the Margaret Sewell School was known locally, and could do some typing, or so she told them. She was appointed as a messenger girl.

'I was the only one, as far as I remember. I used to have to go into these beautiful offices where a senior clerk would give me the post to take round all the departments, and also deliver messages and notices.'

Dulcie was given white overalls and a cap, like the girls on the line, even though she did none of the packing. Going round, she always felt slightly sick in her stomach when she was delivering to the chocolate department because of the smell.

She and her mother, who was still only working part-time, used to come back on the workers bus together which left from outside the main gates of the factory.

For the next four years, Dulcie quite enjoyed her job as a messenger girl. Being able to move around, unlike Ivy and the girls on the production line, she got to know lots of people, one of whom was Eric Wallace. She was exactly the same age as him and when she arrived at Carr's in 1954 she often played tennis with Eric at the Carr's sports ground on Newtown Road.

The reason why Ivy and Dulcie and so many other people of that vintage did know Eric Wallace was that later he became famous. Well, famous in Carlisle. A household face, in fact. Not many Carr's workers over the decades seem to have gone on to other careers, other excitements.

During his ten years working at Carr's, Eric had got involved in his spare time with amateur dramatics. On his days off he studied for his O levels at the Carlisle Technical College and eventually he went on to study at Durham University. He then returned to Carlisle and joined the fledgling Border TV – the smallest of the ITV regional TV companies, founded in 1961, which covered Cumberland, Westmorland, the south of Scotland and the Isle of Man. It had its own studios in Carlisle and its evening local news programme *Lookaround* became immensely popular. Border also created many programmes that appeared on the ITV network, such as *Mr and Mrs*, presented by Derek Batey, who also worked at Border. The studios were closed in 2009, though since 2013 there has been 30 minutes of regional news coming from new premises in Carlisle as ITV Border. But the old Border TV company lives on in the memories of most Cumbrians, especially memories of Eric Wallace who was greatly loved. He died in 2004, aged 66.

Dulcie says she didn't go out with Eric. He was just a good friend at work. At the time they were at Carr's together, and playing the odd game of tennis, he had his eye on another pretty girl in the office. 'Oh there were loads of good-looking girls at Carr's at that time.' Including Dulcie herself, with her bubbly hair and bubbly personality.

However, after four years, Dulcie began to find the life of a messenger girl at Carr's a bit too quiet for her liking.

'The offices seem so old-fashioned, very dignified I know, with mahogany everywhere, but not much talking. I used to see Allen Carr and he would say good morning. I didn't speak to him, but I knew who he was, one of the Carrs.'

Allen Carr was now the chairman. He was one of Jonathan Dodgson Carr's great-grandsons, the latest in a long line to run the family firm.

Jonathan Dodgson Carr had three brothers, two sons and three daughters who in turn had large families, many of whom came into the firm. His younger brother John, however, left the Carlisle firm very early on, around 1858, and joined Peek Freans, a rival biscuit company in London as a partner, eventually becoming in charge. The reason for this is not known, whether there had been a row or something else.

J.D. was a dynamic innovator and a strong personality, convinced he knew the direction in which he wanted his firm to grow and expand. By 1850, the firm owned four flour mills and had created two depots, one in Liverpool and one in London, plus of course their Caldewgate factory. Overseas, they had agents in America, Africa and in most countries of the Empire.

The canal, which had been so vital in the early years, had finally closed in 1853, but by this time Carr's had five of their own ships. They had a ketch called *Swallow* plus four steamships *Swift*, *Surprise*, *Eden* and *Nith* – the last two named after two of the Solway rivers, one flowing through Carlisle and the other Dumfries. Carr's operated their fleet from Cumbrian ports, such as Silloth and Maryport, sending their biscuits to Liverpool, London and the world, giving Carr's alternative transport and independence in case of any railway problems.

But trains were now the main and most important form of transport. Carlisle had become a major railway town, with a brand-spanking-new station, the Citadel, which opened in 1847, built by Sir William Tite in the style of a Tudor palace and still one of the most handsome buildings in Carlisle. Carlisle was on the direct mainline route up from London to Glasgow, and also for getting across from the west coast to the north-east, and was one of the busiest and most important railway centres in the country. By 1876, Citadel station was a terminus for seven different railway companies – London and North-Western, Midland, North Eastern, Caledonian, North British, Glasgow and South-Western, Maryport and Carlisle. No town in the UK could boast that they had more railway companies. All of this helped Carr's to whizz their products around Britain and the world.

Carr's also managed to keep up their public relations coups, building on the granting of their Royal Warrant with a series of other eye-catching achievements during the nineteenth century. They were always quick to dispatch specially made long-lasting dried biscuits whenever there were famines in the Highlands, or supplying rations to Arctic expeditions to one of the poles or to British soldiers out defending the four corners of the Empire.

They entered competitions in the UK and Europe and won endless awards, which naturally they listed on their advertising, and had their wares displayed and on sale at major national events.

This had started back in 1851 when Jonathan Dodgson Carr secured the contract to supply biscuits to the refreshments rooms at the Great Exhibition in London. He created a special Exhibition biscuit, which was first tried out in his family home, with all his children taking bites and giving their opinion. It doesn't appear, from the recipe, to have been much different from their other sweet biscuits of the time, but of course having the name Exhibition biscuit stamped on it made people want to try it.

The firm received some unexpected but wonderful publicity in 1879 at the battle of Rorke's Drift during the Anglo–Zulu war. A handful of English soldiers managed to hold off three hundred Zulu warriors by building a barricade – made out of biscuit tins. No photographs exist of this legendary incident, nor is there proof that the biscuits were actually from Carr's, but Carr's claimed that the biscuits were theirs, as they had supplied them to the troops. Illustrations appeared in the London press and scale models were built, in which you can clearly see the name Carr's. So some good PR work had been done behind the scenes.

A booklet produced by Carr's in 1902, ostensibly a guide to Carlisle but really about Carr's, boasts

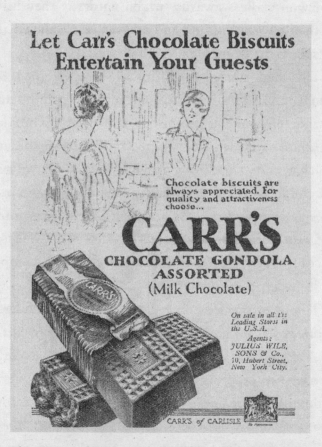

This Carr's advertisement from the 1920s shows that Carr's biscuits were by now being exported to America, as well as many other countries around the globe

how famous the firm had become. 'A household word throughout the civilised world and, we may almost say, throughout the semi-civilised world, for we learn that an agency has recently been opened in Khartoum!'

The story is illustrated by a photograph of a group of armed native warriors standing in awe before a tin of Carr's biscuits. The credit on the photo states that it was from the expedition to Somaliland by H.W. Seton-Karr. Sir Henry Seton-Karr was a well-known late Victorian explorer and also an MP. Presumably Carr's had supplied him with biscuits, on condition he sent them a snap.

That same booklet describes the joy of visiting Carr's biscuits, having an organised tour, and tells you what you might see, such as the Icing and Decorating Room.

A small army of girls, all in neat overalls, are busily engaged in decorating or icing biscuits. Messrs Carr and Co have made an important feature of these goods and their Café Noir, Finger Creams, Lemon Creams, Windsor Wafers are known and appreciated all over the world. In the Packing and Forwarding Departments, the biscuits are packed by nimble-fingered girls into their various tins covered with artistic covers and packed into cases in which they are despatched

to customers at home and abroad. Upwards of
300 kinds of biscuits are manufactured – fastidi-
ous indeed must be the epicure who fails to find
among them something to suit his taste.

The notion of epicures being Carr's biscuit eaters is an attractive one, but their biscuits were indeed appealing to all strata of society. When the *Titanic* went down in 1912, they were munching away at Carr's Table Water Biscuits in the first-class lounges. (Another connection with Carlisle was the chief engineer, Joseph Bell, who died in the disaster, came from the village of Farlam, just outside Carlisle.)

Jonathan Dodgson Carr remained in day-to-day control of Carr's till 1884, by which time the company had well over a thousand workers at their Carlisle factory.

Girls of the 'forwarding staff' in 1929, in their working coats and caps, the boxes neatly stacked up ready for dispatch.

He had taken part in several national campaigns, notably a fight to repeal the Corn Laws, which restricted free trade and made the import of cereal crops from abroad very expensive. When this was successful, he had created for himself a specially made silk waistcoat. It had ears of corn woven into the pattern along with the word FREE. (Today, the waistcoat is on show at Tullie House Museum in Carlisle.) All his life, though, he remained a local rather than a national figure, big in biscuit circles, admired by his peers, but still living modestly in Carlisle. He walked to work each day, tall, hefty, towering and bearded, still personally involved with all aspects of his biscuit factory and his flourmills.

One day, when purchasing grain at the market in Carlisle, he discovered that he had been given two more bags than he had bought. He asked the police to trace the person who had mistakenly given him too much, but they were unable to do so. Six months later, he went to the chief constable and placed a sum of money on his desk. 'What's this for?' asked the chief constable.

'It's the money I got for the flour I milled from the two extra bags. Do what thou likes with it but it isn't mine.'

A description of him in 1861 records that he had a 'massive form and benevolent countenance'. One of his grandsons, Frederick Carr, later remembered how he would perform feats of strength when going round the factory or his mills.

'He lifted a twenty-stone sack of flour on to his back, took two other sacks, one under each arm, walked the length of the mill and replaced the sacks. The total weight must have been forty stone, but he did it easily. After dusting the flour off himself, he laughed and asked if anyone would like to have a try.'

Despite being such a progressive and creative businessman, making use of steam power, immediately seeing all the possibilities in the new and wonderful railways, and exploiting any opportunities for publicity, he did come a cropper when he invested heavily in some tin mines in Cornwall. He and some friends he had encouraged to join him in the investment lost all their money. He had to sell his large house in Stanwix, Carlisle, and downsize till he made up his losses.

Towards the end of his life, he gave up being a Quaker, supposedly in support of two of his sons who had left – possibly asked to leave – the Society of Friends. J.D. then joined a local Presbyterian church in Carlisle, where he was active and still involved in many good works till the end of his life.

Jonathan Dodson Carr had a stroke in April 1884 and died a week later, aged seventy-seven. Over 500 people attended his funeral and he was buried in Carlisle cemetery. He left behind his wife, three sons and two daughters and seventeen grandchildren, of which twelve were boys. More than enough to carry on the family firm into the next century.

Chapter 5
Dulcie

Dulcie, despite being on 'good morning' terms with Allen Carr, Jonathan Dodgson's great-grandson, decided that after four years as a messenger girl at Carr's she had had enough. She didn't seem to be getting anywhere, so she slowly came to the conclusion that she should try for a proper office job.

In 1959, she managed to secure one at Rickerby's, a long-established Cumbrian firm that sold and repaired agricultural machinery. While there she started going out with Bob, who was eight years older than her, tall dark and handsome.

'I didn't know what his job was. All he seemed to do was walk around. I think maybe he had something to do with lawnmowers.'

Dulcie had gone out with quite a few boys since the age of fifteen, putting on her best clothes for the occasion. 'I liked shopping at Richards and Eve Brown. My favourites were a circular felt skirt, tight black straight skirt, and white broderie anglaise blouse worn with a cameo broach. I longed for a Hebe Sports suit, but they were far too expensive.

'I had nylons, but I didn't wear a corset, which my mother did. But I do remember wearing a Playtex foundation garment. You had to put talcum powder in to help you get it on.

'I didn't go to the hairdresser much, only to have it cut or perhaps a bubble perm. I had it permed all over, curly all over, and sometimes bleached the front with peroxide.

'Rock Hudson was my idea of a handsome man. I couldn't believe it when later we found out he was gay.'

Boyfriends would often take Dulcie to the pub, where she would have a Babycham or perhaps a shandy, feeling daring. Pubs were male strongholds in the post-war years, and fairly dour and cheerless, with nothing to eat. Old men in flat caps sat in corners with their whippets and glared at any young people who came in, especially young women, considering them to be no better than they should be. Pubs were not considered fun places, but were meant for serious drinkers only. Especially in Carlisle.

'I don't think I ever went to a pub on my own. Girls didn't. In fact, I hardly went to pubs. It wasn't something you did. The only time might be on a Saturday night when I went to the dance at the Cameo Ballroom in Botchergate. I would get a pass out and perhaps go with a boy, and sometimes just a girlfriend, to the Cumberland pub nearby. We'd have a Babycham and then come back and carry on dancing.'

Carlisle was unique in England, perhaps in the whole world, outside communist Russia, for its system of public houses – for they were all state controlled. The landlords were civil servants. The buildings were owned by the government. All profits went to the Chancellor of the Exchequer.

This strange arrangement began during the First World War when massive munitions works were being created at Gretna, about ten miles away on the Scottish border. On Saturday evenings, up to 5,000 workers, most of them Irish navvies, would come into Carlisle on the train for the sole purpose of getting drunk. They would pour out of the Citadel station and head for the nearest pub where the landlord would already have lined up a hundred glasses of whisky on the counters. They usually had a brief drinking period, because of the train times or their shifts, so had to get as much down as possible in a short time. The result was bedlam.

'Drunkenness among munitions workers,' said Lloyd George, Minister of Munitions, 'is doing more damage in the war than all the German submarines put together.'

So it was decided to nationalise all the pubs and hotels in Carlisle and the surrounding district. Only a small, select handful of licensed places stayed in private hands, notably the Crown and Mitre. Navvies would not have gone there anyway. Grocers lost their licence to sell beer and spirits, so you could only buy alcohol in the state-owned premises – and at very restricted opening times.

Some pubs did offer alcohol for sale to take away, but this usually consisted of a cubbyhole in the wall at the end of the bar. When you knocked on it, and eventually someone appeared, and you asked to buy a bottle to take out, they would usually say 'sorry, pet, we're closed'.

On the other hand, the drinks were slightly cheaper in the Carlisle and District State Management area than elsewhere as they had their own brewery, producing their own brands of beers and stouts, and also their own whisky, Border Blend.

It all came to an end in 1971, when the pubs were all sold off. Their demise was hardly mourned by most locals. Today, however, the story of Carlisle State Management has become an interesting small footnote in England's social history. Books have been written about this period and in Carlisle there is a permanent exhibition to the State Management in the city museum at Tullie House. The bottles and beer mats had their own logos and artwork, while the pubs themselves were mostly custom built and were interesting architecturally, with their own individual style.

All our young women, when growing up, should they have been bold enough to go for a drink on their own or even when invited by a beau, would have been unaware of the history and how unusual the local pubs were – and they considered them a fairly unattractive proposition for a night out. 'I actually worked in a state-management pub at one time, just for a few months,' said Dulcie. 'It was the Ship Inn at Thursby, as a barmaid. It was quite easy really as of course there were no bar meals.'

Dulcie, suitably dressed up, used to go dancing at the Cameo a lot, and went to the Market Hall when any of the big bands of the day were performing. She remembers going to see Eric Delaney, a drummer and bandleader, born 1924, who was very popular in the 1950s and '60s, appearing on the radio and the Royal Variety Show.

'There was another famous band I went to with a friend of mine, Syd Lawrence and his Big Band. My friend went home with one of them, took him to her house. I asked her why she did this when he was so much older and not very attractive, though he was nice enough. She said it was because he had a big car. It wasn't a romantic interlude. Just ships that pass in the night.'

Her own romance with Bob was going well, till it came to the annual Rickerby staff dance. Dulcie wanted him to take her – but he refused.

'He said, "I see all these people at work all the time, why do I want to see them at a dance?"

'So, just to show him he wasn't the only pebble on the beach, I went off and married someone else.

'I had met this boy earlier at a dance and he was a soldier. I decided to marry him. My mam was very upset, in fact really furious, but I said I'm going to, don't care what you say. So I did. And me mam did give me a church wedding and a do at the Co-Op.

'After two weeks, the marriage was over. It was a stupid mistake. I was a silly girl, only twenty-two. What actually happened was that after two weeks he was sent abroad, to Germany. I thought to myself that's it. Once he's gone, he's gone.

'I probably was a bit hard-faced in them days, but you were considered a scarlet woman in the fifties and sixties if you lived with a man you were not married to. So marrying seemed the thing to do. My mother was disgusted with me.'

She then got back with Bob, her real love, and they soon moved in together, managing to rent a flat, pretending they were a married couple.

Dulcie then got pregnant, and had to confess it to her mother, going into the Fusehill Maternity Hospital to have the baby.

'I had to tell my mother that when she comes to visit me, be sure to ask for Mrs Pitt, a name I'd just made up.'

Louise was born in 1965. A year later she and Bob did get married, at a register office, and moved into a rented house in Nelson Street. By then they had another daughter, Elizabeth, born in 1966.

In 1969, Bob had a fancy to move out into the country, though Dulcie was never keen, preferring the bright lights and fun of the city. He bought a derelict farm and barn near Thursby, about six miles from Carlisle, for a bargain price of £3,000. His fantasy was to do up all the outhouses, convert and sell them.

Dulcie and her husband had just the two children. 'With my first husband, we did use condoms now and again, but I hated them. With Bob, I wanted children, so didn't bother much. Then when we'd had the girls, I did go on the Pill for a while, but that was really to regulate my periods. I was always told the Pill was bad for you, if you stayed on it too long.

'The best form of contraception is of course "GERROFF!" You know, Gerroff, your time's up.'

When Louise was aged five, Dulcie and her husband were out with her one day when she ran away, just down a street, and they shouted after her – but she took no notice. They shouted again – and she appeared not to hear anything they had said.

'We took her to the doctor and he says to me, "Does she look deaf?" I said I don't know. What does deaf look like? Anyway she was sent for tests – and was pronounced to be profoundly deaf, and had been since birth. There was a great enquiry about this, how on earth had she slipped through the net.

'The school in Thursby knew she had problems speaking, but not what the problem was. A social worker had told me she could be autistic, but it might get better.

'I suppose we had suspected something was wrong. For some time when we had made noises we realised she didn't seem to hear them. But we had no experience of anyone being deaf. No one in our families had been deaf. We didn't understand what deaf meant, what happened, how it affected you.

'It was very upsetting when it got confirmed but then we just felt we had to get on with it, that was how it was. We had to live with it, hope for the best, see how it developed.'

Louise didn't get better and aged six until the age of fifteen she was sent away to the Northern Counties Deaf School, a boarding school. It did help her to read and write – but she hated it.

'Every time she came home for the weekend she would accuse me of not loving her. She said, "Elizabeth sleeps here seven nights a week and I only sleep here two nights a week. You just want to get rid of me." I had to explain to her it was for her own good. She could never learn anything if she stayed at home and went to the ordinary school.'

When Elizabeth, her younger daughter, was seven and established at the village primary school, Dulcie decided to go back to Carr's. She took a shift that went from 9.30 to 3.30, which fitted in with having young children. The work was on the line, packing biscuits, as her mother was still doing, but it was an unusual shift whereby you moved round all the time, filling in for girls who were on their half-hour breakfast or lunch break.

'It didn't have a name – just the 9.30 shift. We were not very popular. The other girls were doing the same job for eight hours at a time, but we just arrived, did it for only half an hour, then we got moved on somewhere else. They said it was because we couldn't cope, we were not good or quick or clever enough to do the same thing for eight hours, which was probably true.'

So, despite the advantage of having been at the Margaret Sewell School, one of the chosen ones, if not quite the first eleven, Dulcie had returned to work at Carr's. And she packed biscuits, just like her mother.

The biscuits which Dulcie was packing included many relatively new lines such as Café Iced, Varsity, Emblem Assorted, Coconut Macaroons, Capri, Lunch, many of them long gone. There is a good full-colour illustration of the current biscuits being produced in the Carr and Company Limited Annual report for the year 1960. A photograph shows some of the girls at work, looking immaculate in their uniforms but also wearing low heels as they stand on what looks like gleaming parquet floor in front of their machines. They are not on the production line but in the accounts office, working a new punched card system, which clearly the company was very proud of.

In the chairman's statement at the front of the 1960 booklet, Allen Carr reveals that while demand for biscuits has remained steady, and turnover has increased by 3 per cent, and that they have installed more labour-saving equipment, there are some worrying factors outside their control, such as currency and import restrictions in several countries, the rising price of cocoa beans and also political changes. He mentions Cuba as a market that has closed. This was due to the Cuban revolution of 1959 when Castro took over and trade relations with the USA and the West generally came to an end. He says that they are now going to try harder in more settled markets, such as Canada, the USA and the West Indies.

But the biggest threat, which had been there since the 1840s, was from rival firms, which was one of the reasons why all biscuit manufacturers were continually trying to think of new, tempting lines to attract the population.

The number of Carr's lines had been jumping all the time, from just two at the beginning in 1839, to twenty by the 1840s. By the 1860s, a retail list of Carr's biscuits, produced for the trade, lists 145 different named varieties. Amazing that they could have produced so many in just one relatively small factory.

The names make fascinating reading, betraying some of the social and political fashions of the times. Captain's Thin is still there, plus digestives and Rich Desserts, but there are lots of names with vaguely royal or aristocratic overtones, such as Albert biscuits, Balmoral, Clarence, Osborne, Prince of Wales and Victoria Drops. Quite a few exotic names have appeared, taken from foreign parts, perhaps inspired by places that had been featured in the newspapers, such as Smyrna, Java, Riviera, Madeira, or the use of foreign words to lend a certain sophistication, such as Croquette, Demi Lune, Eclaire, and Pain D'Amandes.

The list includes Garibaldi biscuits, which were named after the Italian general, Giuseppe Garibaldi, who made a visit to Tynemouth in 1854. He received even more enthusiastic attention when he visited London in 1864. Garibaldi biscuits were created in 1861 by Peek Frean, not by Carr's, but every rival biscuit manufacturer soon added them, or something similar, to their portfolio. The inspiration behind the Garibaldis was in fact John Carr, the younger brother of J.D., almost twenty years younger, who had left Carr's to run Peek Freans.

Garibaldis, which consist of two thin oblong biscuits with a filling of currants, are still going strong.

They often get a name check in TV shows and films, showing how popular they have remained.

Abernethy biscuits were also on the list – named after a Scottish doctor called John Abernethy. He suggested them to a local bakery and restaurant where he regularly had lunch, saying they would be good for the digestion. They were adapted from the old hard tack ship's biscuit, but more palatable.

It's interesting how several nineteenth-century doctors managed to create biscuits that have lived on to this day, usually doctors who were interested in healthy living, thinking up biscuits which might be good for their patients to eat. Bath Olivers were created by Dr William Oliver of Bath in 1750, which possibly makes them one of the oldest named biscuits. He bequeathed the recipe to his coachman, a Mr Atkins, plus £100 and ten sacks of best flour, who immediately set himself up as a biscuit maker.

In the USA in 1829, Graham Crackers were named after a real person, the Reverend Sylvester Graham, a Presbyterian minister. He saw them as part of every-one's healthy diet and believed they would help to suppress carnal thoughts or, even worse, the horrors of self-abuse. Other people over the decades have also believed that the right sort of wholesome food would lead to wholesome habits, such as John Harvey Kellogg, when he created his bland cornflakes.

The worldwide attraction of biscuits has, however, tended to lie more in the joy of biscuits rather than any medical effects. It's the stimulation and pleasure of the sugar rush, plus the addition of fruit, chocolate, spices and other ingredients which has such appeal, and why ingenious manufacturers are still constantly thinking up ways to add to the basic biscuity taste and contents.

Dry biscuits, crackers in all their various forms, the type that originated from the other historic source of biscuit, have always had their fans – nowadays usually eaten with the addition of cheese.

Carr's, like all the manufacturers, have always paid attention to producing both sweet and savoury biscuits, catering for the two basic human tastes, and were lucky that their Table Water Biscuits went on to prove so popular with all classes.

The Duke of Wellington was known to keep a tin of Abernethy biscuits on his desk, ready to nibble them in times of stress or boredom or just greed. In the nineteenth-century novels written by Anthony Trollope, the women on train journeys keep themselves going on sweet biscuits. Station and railway refreshment was at the time rather inadequate.

Oscar Wilde, when he was interned in Reading gaol in 1897, managed to get smuggled in a supply of Ginger Nut biscuits. He had fallen in love with them three years earlier when he had made a tour of the Huntley & Palmers factory in Reading. Biscuits do go with all occasions.

Chapter 6

Dorothy

Country girl Dorothy as a teenager

Ivy and Dulcie were council-house kids, born and brought up on one of Carlisle's large estates, just a mile or so from the Carr's factory, like the majority of the post-war Carr's workers. Dorothy was different. She was a country girl.

Dorothy was born as the Second World War broke out – on 31 August 1939 – on a small farm near the village of Sebergham, about ten miles from Carlisle.

One of the factors that has always made Carlisle feel like an isolated town is that for roughly fifty miles around it is mainly rural, with no other similar-sized towns. Going west, you eventually reach the old West

Cumbrian mining areas of Whitehaven and Workington some forty miles away. Going fifty miles east you hit Newcastle. Going a hundred miles due north, you eventually reach Glasgow.

It has meant for two centuries at least that 'country folk' from a large and scattered catchment area have been traipsing into Carlisle each day for work, for shopping, for entertainment or for secondary schooling.

Naturally some of the city slickers of Carlisle have always felt superior to their country cousins, considering them slow and old-fashioned, with straw sticking out of their ears. A gross libel, of course.

One of the remarkable features of Cumbria's home-grown multi-millionaires who became nationally well known has been their rural origins. They include John Laing the builder (originally from Sebergham); Eddie Stobart of the lorry firm (Hesket Newmarket); the Denning family who run the Westmorland service station on the M6 and Reghed (Shap) and the Rayner family who began Lakeland, the kitchenware firm (Windermere). And of course John Dodgson Carr from Kendal.

Dorothy's family were rural but not quite of such a business bent. Her father Joe, who was living on a rented smallholding when Dorothy was born, did later acquire a small farm of around fifty acres bought by his father, but instead of using this chance to expand, he gave it up and his father took it back.

Joe then reverted to being a hired hand, an agricultural labourer, who moved around the Sebergham, Dalston and Hesket Newmarket area when Dorothy and her older sister Margaret were growing up, living in a sequence of farm cottages that came with his job.

'He didn't like managing things. He liked being out in the open all the time. And I think he was a bit like me, taking things easy and not wanting too much stress, but he was a lovely man.'

Dorothy's earliest memory dates back to when she was three, in the summer of 1942 when they were living near Hesket. A Lancaster bomber had come down, trying to limp home after being shot at over Germany, and had crashed into the side of a high fell.

'We all set off to go and find it, my mam and dad and my sister. We'd never seen a plane before, so we were very excited. It seemed to take ages, and we must have been walking for two hours. I ended up on my dad's shoulders. We could see the plane clearly on the fellside, but it was hard to get at.

'The crew had survived, somehow, and been taken to hospital by the time we arrived, but there was some RAF and police guarding it.

'My dad lifted me up and put me on the wing. I was so scared! I think I cried. I thought the plane was going to take off.'

Dorothy had bright red hair – unlike her mother and father. '"Where has she come from?" People used to say. I did have an aunt with red hair and when my father grew a moustache, it always came out ginger. I liked having red hair. Didn't bother me. The usual remark when I was at school was, "Left out in the rain, were you, and gone all rusty?"'

The war had little effect on their family rural life. They had plenty to eat as her father grew potatoes, turnips, apples, corn, wheat, barley and kept a few cows while their mother had hens.

'But every little inch had to be cultivated for the war effort, even bits that had never been used, which was why me dad had to grow some wheat, which he had never done. They came round inspecting you. One year the inspector refused my dad's wheat, said it wasn't up to standard. My mother maintained they were just saying it – they had too much already. There was nothing wrong with his wheat, so she said.

'I suppose we were lucky, living on a farm in wartime, as we had things like eggs all the time, from our own hens, unlike people living in town only being allowed one a week, or whatever it was. When we had any spare, Mam sold them to the Egg Marketing Board. It gave her a bit of money.

'My father also kept a few pigs, so we usually had plenty of bacon and ham, but there were wartime restrictions about pig keeping. Depending on how many ration books you had in the house, and we had four, that decided how many pigs you could kill a year. We were allowed two.

'We didn't kill the pigs ourselves, that was not allowed, it had to be a registered butcher. He would come to the farm twice a year and kill one of our pigs. When I was little I was quite fascinated by it, but when I was a young girl, I hated the sound of the pig squealing. I used to run away and hide in the fields when I heard the pig squealing. Everyone thought it was very funny.

'We got groceries once a fortnight from a van, the Co-op van, which came to the lane end or we might go to the village shop, but that was a bit of a trail. Mainly we had very plain food.

'It was always a roast on Sunday, beef mainly. Next day we had cold meat, then it was made into a shepherd's pie or hot pot. The roast could be made to last up to half the week. We usually had a pudding, either rice pudding or stewed fruit, just what was in season.

'My father didn't cook, but he said he could. And my mother said he could. But I don't actually remember him ever doing any. He thought it was woman's work, so if there were any around, he let them do it. Anyway, he was out all day in the fields, not like people on shift work in factories who would come home at a regular set time. So Mam did all the cooking. And I would help her – because I liked it. We always sat down together, at the table, and ate together, even if we had to wait for my dad to come in from the fields.

'I had no likes and dislikes. I liked everything. Well, it was plain, natural food, so you couldn't dislike it, could you. Fried tomatoes, that was the only thing I wasn't so keen on. I like tomatoes, but plain and uncooked.

'My parents never drank in the house, not that I ever saw. My father might go out to the pub for a drink now and again, but not often. He didn't have the money. But there was usually a bottle of rum and a bottle of whisky in the house. I don't remember anyone ever drinking it though. The rum was used for cooking – for making rum butter or rum sauce for the Christmas pudding.

'We also had a lot of soups and broths, anything like that to warm us up. Oh, it was so cold in them days, the winters were terrible. We had no central heating of course, or any sort of heating, apart from the one fire. We had no gas and no electricity, with living out in the country, not till we moved into Dalston. For most of my childhood the cooking was done on an open fire, with a range, using coal or logs. For light we had paraffin lamps. The radio ran on batteries, which were so expensive and huge.

'It was so cold we used to sit with blankets over us, even in front of the open fire. That's what we did most evening in the winter, huddle round the fire in the lamplight.

'When you went to bed, you put on as many layers and as many blankets as you could, as of course there was no heat in the bedrooms either. Rubber hot-water bottles were hard to get during the war. I think rubber was going to the war effort. So you used a stone hot-water bottle. We also had an aluminium one at one time. It was a like a Thermos flask. You filled it with hot water. If you touched it with your bare hands or feet you would scream. I used to put it inside one of my dad's old socks and take it to bed. You would literally burn your feet if the sock wasn't there.

In the morning, it was agony. You tried not to stand on the lino floor with your bare feet. Otherwise you would freeze to death, or be stuck to the lino till spring-time. And of course the windows were frozen on the inside when you woke up.

'So yes, that was one of the bad things about living out in the country in the war, with no gas and electricity.'

Around Carlisle, and in many other rural areas, there were prisoner-of-war camps, which provided cheap labour on the local farms. Dorothy remembers some Czech farm labourers working with her father, but assumes they were refugees from war-torn Europe, not POWs.

Her father served in the Home Guard from its inception in 1940 till 1944. Anthony Eden, Secretary of State for War, had announced its creation in May 1940, saying that any males between the ages of seventeen and sixty-five who were not eligible so far for military service should join up and help to defend the nation from possible invasion. Within a week, 250,000 had joined. By July, the total was 1.5 million. The vast majority were middle-aged, hence the title *Dad's Army*. There is a myth that no Home Guard soldier ever fired a shot in anger, but in fact in the big towns, such as London during the Battle of Britain, they helped to man anti-aircraft guns. The first casualty inflicted by anyone in the Home Guard was on Tyneside in 1943 when a Home Guard gunner brought down a German plane.

Dorothy's father served for the whole of the war and she remembers that he wore a uniform, carried a rifle and rose to the rank of corporal. In rural Cumbria of course there was little call to man anti-aircraft batteries.

'But he did get a certificate for map reading – which my mother always laughed at. She couldn't understand it as she said he never had any sense of direction.'

Dorothy has kept all her father's Home Guard mementos, his certificates, badges, bits of his uniform, and also a very nicely printed message of thanks from the Lieutenant Colonel of the 3rd Cumberland Battalion, HG of the Border Regiment, presented in 1945, when the war was over.

There are many officers and men I hope to see again. Some may however move to other places and our ways will part. To these I say 'Thank you, goodbye and good luck. To those who remain in Cumberland, thank you and au revoir.'

The commanding officer who signed this touching card was Lt. Col. RN Carr, MC – Ronald Carr (1894–1967), another one of J.D.'s grandsons.

He is rather overshadowed in the Carr family saga by another, slightly older grandson, Theodore Carr, who after Jonathan Dodgson himself is always reckoned to be the most innovative and energetic of the subsequent Carr dynasty.

It was Theodore Carr (1866–1931) who is credited with establishing what became known as Carr's Table Water Biscuits. Some Americans claim they had invented a similar dried cracker earlier, but of course the origins of such biscuits go back to the hard tack used by sailors.

Carr's had from almost the beginning been success-fully producing a dry biscuit version called Captain's Thin, but it was in 1890 that Theodore managed to create what he called a Table Water Biscuit. It was one third as thin as normal dried biscuits but delicate and lighter in colour as it had not been baked in the ovens for as long. It was a complicated process to get it right, and not end up with a pile of crumbs. The name 'crackers', as originated in the USA, had come from the fact that in the baking process, it did tend to crack and pop. Table Water Biscuits are made simply from flour and water, hence the name, with no fats or sugars added, and the reference to table suggested it should be displayed on the dining table, ready to be scoffed when the cheese course arrived.

In 1901 Theodore launched the Café Noir biscuit, aimed at more sophisticated tastes, which proved extremely popular. In 1906 he helped invent what became known as the Baker-Carr machine, which iced biscuits in one tenth of the time it had previously taken by hand.

Theodore was also an MP and a car fanatic, building Carlisle's first ever steam-driven motorcar in 1896, creating clouds of steam as he tore around the country lanes scattering terrified locals and ignoring all rules and regulations.

Ronald Carr, his younger cousin, aged just thirty-seven when his older cousin Theodore died, had never been expected to do much, in life or in the family firm. He had been a sensitive, delicate young man, educated at Repton and Cambridge.

By now the Carrs had not just ceased to be Quakers, but were keen to send their children to the best public schools, universities and regiments, which traditionally Quakers had shunned, being against hierarchies or any sorts of oaths of allegiance. One reason Jonathan Dodgson never sent his own sons to boarding school was that he heard that in the sixth form they were allowed what was known as 'small beers'. He was, of course, strictly teetotal all his life. Young Ronald Carr had disliked being dragged round the factory as a child, and was determined not to go into biscuits. But when the First World War began, he joined up and served with distinction, as did several of the Carrs – a sure sign that their Quaker pacifist origins had been long forgotten.

Aged only twenty-two, Ronald Carr was awarded the Military Cross for bravery. On the same day, Stanley Carr, son of Theodore, was killed. After the war, Ronald felt it was his duty to serve the family firm. He was an active director for many years, eventually becoming chairman. He was considered pretty tough, keen to drive the firm forward and make it as profitable as possible.

During both world wars, Carr's factory kept going, but of course production was limited and controlled. A lot of the wartime work in the nation's factories was secret, especially anything to do with munitions, but Ronald Carr in his 1946 Christmas message to the workers revealed exactly what they had been doing during the recent war years.

'Our fortunate geographical positions enabled us to do much what other firms were unable to tackle. We packed curry powder and organised production of camouflage nets, both very sneezy jobs. We made special packs of biscuits for the Pacific war and tons of vitamin chocolate. It tasted awful, but doubtless it served its purpose. I think it might be said that the firm met all the demands made upon it and rendered good service.'

Dorothy today still treasures the signed card from Ronald Carr, which was given to her father at the end of the war when she was aged six and still at primary school.

She was at Sebergham village school when she sat the Eleven Plus, but like Ivy, it was a bit of non-event and she doesn't remember much about it.

'I wasn't very brainy, as well as being lazy. My mam used to say I didn't know anything. I couldn't concentrate at school. I wanted to be out in the fields, watching my father ploughing with his horses. He didn't have any tractors during the war, and nobody had a car. I used to like sitting on his turnip drill behind the horses. I knew exactly where each cow should go in the byre, but my sister didn't. She wasn't interested in the farm.'

Only one girl in Dorothy's year passed the Eleven Plus, but the year before her younger sister Margaret had rather surprised the family when she passed the Merit for the high school.

Dorothy went for a while to the little primary school in Hesket Newmarket, where in her class was Eddie Stobart, senior – father of Edward, the one who went on to build up Eddie's little local agricultural firm into a massive transport organisation.

In 1952, Dorothy aged thirteen, a solemn but open-faced, open-hearted girl, moved to Wigton Secondary Modern in the small town of Wigton, the home of Melvyn Bragg, another Cumbrian who did good, but he was at Nelson Tomlinson, Wigton's grammar school.

Wigton Secondary Modern was in a brand-new building that could double up as a hospital. They had a uniform, but Dorothy was excused having to wear one as she had arrived late and was just going to be there for two years. 'It seemed enormous, after the one-class village schools I had been at. I didn't know anyone. They were all strangers. But anyway, you just get on with it, don't you, as best you can, sort of style.'

She left school in the summer of 1954, just a month before turning fifteen. She looked for work, knowing the chances were that if she was lucky, it would be in Carlisle. There were few jobs at the time for young women in country areas – and even fewer today.

She wasn't fazed by the thought of the big city, having been to it regularly over the years with her family.

'Me and my mam and sister used to come in on a Saturday for shopping, leaving really early and coming back quite late. It was a big outing for us and we usually ended up having some tea at the country café. Dad had no car, so we came on the bus.

'I used to think Carlisle people were better off than us. Not just more money but they had better things.

We always thought the best stuff in the covered market or the shops had gone by the time we got there. Things like new clothes, new fashions, they had disappeared by the time we had even heard of them.

'The accents were a bit different. They seemed a bit more intelligent, or advanced, let's say. I noticed that the children were allowed to go and run messages to the shops or go on the bus from about the age of eight. Me and my sister were not allowed to go on the bus alone till we were ten or eleven. And then only if we were together.

'When we got a bit older, we all used to go into Carlisle as a family once a week in the evenings, to go to the cinema. I loved cowboy films and thrillers. We had chips afterwards on the way home. It seemed so exciting, going into Carlisle.'

Dorothy's first job was in a small confectionery shop, Richardson's in Longsowerby, on another of Carlisle's council estates. Mrs Richardson ran the bakery side with Dorothy and another girl, while Mr Richardson and his son ran the shop part. They didn't bake bread, that was bought in, but made a wide range of tea cakes, scones, shortbreads and cakes, baked in their own bakery.

Dorothy came in every day to work on the early bus, seven o'clock, from Dalston, near where her father was now working, along with the other early workers. 'I loved the bus ride, going down Dalston road as we got into Carlisle, and seeing all the big houses.'

Her starting wage was £2 7s 3d. She loved the job, staying there thirteen years, till the Richardsons retired. She then spent eight years as a machinist in a textile factory, Morton Sundour, machining curtains and bath mats, till that factory closed and it moved to Bolton.

In 1976, she was out of work for three months, worried that she wouldn't get another job. She was still living with her family who had by now moved into Carlisle. Her father – with his father's help – had managed to buy a small house in Wood Street. Her sister Margaret had got married and moved to Gloucester.

Through the Job Centre, Dorothy was told there might be a vacancy at Carr's. She went for the interview, where naturally they gave her nails a good inspection.

'The man who saw me, Tommy Walker, was mostly interested in whether I had any of my family working here. I got the impression that was what got you in, or at least gave you a better chance. I had nobody, coming from a line of farming people. But anyway, they took me on. I was thrilled, after being out of work.

'The woman who trained me was Ivy Graham, a few years older than me. She seemed to have been there for ever. She was very nice. Can't say anything against Ivy. And my charge hand was called Jean. She had an accent I had never heard before.'

Chapter 7

Jean

Jean as a young woman

Dorothy's, Dulcie's and Ivy's memories of wartime Carlisle and Cumbria are nothing compared with Jean's wartime memories. But then Jean, unlike the other three, had grown up somewhere enemy air raids were frequent, and bombs and deaths were a reality.

Jean was born in West Derby, Liverpool on 3 July 1936. And she was born a twin – though it was only many years later that she discovered this fact. The other baby was born dead. She doesn't even know whether it was a boy or a girl. It was her grandmother who told her about it when she was a teenager, but never revealed the baby's sex, and Jean never asked.

'All I know about my birth is that I was born very small, premature, and they put me in a shoe box with cotton wool round me.'

Her dad, at the time of her birth, was working in a furniture factory and then moved to a bakery. Her mother, so she was told later, had been an actress and singer and once went to Paris with a production of the *Pirates of Penzance*. 'She was called Babs Melia, that was her stage name, she was really called Margaret. My grandmother told me this, but I don't know how correct it was.'

The reason for the mystery was due to the fact that her mother died, aged twenty-seven in May 1940, when little Jean was only three, so her memories of her mother are few and faint.

'My mother had TB. I do remember being taken to see her in hospital but they wouldn't let me in. Children were not allowed in hospitals in those days. I sat outside on a bench with my dad while my grandma went in to see my mother.

'I remember being lifted up by someone, I don't know who it was, so I could see my mother in her coffin. I don't remember at the time being scared or worried or thinking anything really, but ever since, whenever anyone in the family or any friend has died, I don't want to see the body. I didn't even look at my own father in his coffin.'

By this time, the war had started and her dad had joined up and gone into the RAF where he flew in a Lancaster bomber as a navigator. He crash-landed once and injured his knee and was in hospital for some time. 'He used to tell me stories of trying to sneak out of the hospital, hiding under the bed, then running out of the door, but they always brought him back.'

By some remote and amazing coincidence, could his crashed Lancaster bomber possibly have been the same one which little Dorothy went to see on the Cumbrian hillside when she was three in 1942? That was the year the Lancaster bomber was introduced, so the dates tie in. Lancasters were the RAF's heavy bombers – 7,377 were built and they did 156,000 sorties during the war years. One of them was modified to carry Barnes Wallis's famous bouncing dam-busting bombs.

After the death of her mother, Jean lived with her grandmother, her father's mother, whom she always called by her nickname of Ninner. Then her father got married again, and Jean was brought back from her gran's to live with her father and her new stepmother, Elsie.

'She didn't like me, I don't know why. She treated me like a slave, making me scrub the front step, scrub the bedroom floors, clean the dishes, go for messages. If I did anything wrong, like come back with the wrong change, she would hit me. Many a time I was black and blue through being beaten.

'The teachers did find out, but did nothing about it. You didn't in those days. There wasn't all the Social Services like today.

'She kept me short of food as well, so my grandmother used to meet me at the school gates and pass me a sandwich or a bottle of lemonade.'

But while Jean was unhappy at home, she enjoyed primary school at Vine Street, and quite liked the war, finding it interesting and exciting, despite all the bombing and destruction going on all around her in Liverpool.

At school when the bombs went off, Jean and all the other pupils would go into the cellars and lie down, each pupil on their own mat. At home, they didn't have a shelter in their house so when the bombs fell they would go into the communal shelters in the street. 'I hated them. They were so smelly and filthy, people used them as lavatories. I would rather have stayed in our house and sheltered under the stairs.

'We were sheltering at home one night when the back door flew open and all the cats of the neighbourhood flew in – terrified by the noise of the bombs. I was alarmed at first, when they burst in, then I had to laugh. It was so funny.

'You never knew what local houses and buildings had been hit till you went out next day. The worst were the whistle bombs, whistling over your head, and you'd be wondering where they would fall. I liked looking up at the sky in the dark, seeing all the criss-crossing lights, with the bombs and barrage balloons and the aeroplanes, trying to work out which were the Germans. You were not supposed to be outside, so the ARP wardens would chase you inside.

'I did enjoy going on the trams next day with my friends into town to see the bomb damage. My step-mother didn't know I was doing this, but four of us would go for a penny ride on the tram. I remember seeing Blacklers, which was a very big posh department store, a bit like Binns in Carlisle, and it had been totally demolished and was still on fire. But they were already setting up makeshift stalls, putting up tarpaulins over the wreckage and selling stuff. Lewis's was bombed – they had a zoo at the back which was wiped out.

'At school you didn't know who would turn up each day, or who had been bombed. I did know two people who got killed by a bomb near us.

'They weren't really trying to bomb us in West Derby, just by accident really. They were heading further on, for the docks and the Pier Head.

'I went down to the Pier Head one day and I saw a German plane stuck in a wall. It was on fire, but I couldn't see if there was a pilot inside, dead or not. It looked so weird, stuck right in the wall of a warehouse.

'I don't remember being scared. Our lives went on as normal really, being kids, having fun, playing games.

I would go to Woolton Woods with my friend and sit by the floral clock and watch our RAF planes landing and taking off at Speke airport.

'Because my dad was in the war, away in the RAF, and my mother was dead, I was treated in a way like an orphan and my grandmother found out I could get free shoes. She took me to the Walker Gallery, which was a very big building. At the back there was a room that had these tables and you lined up. My gran gave my details, I got weighed and measured, then I was given a free pair of shoes. In the summer you got free sandals.

'We also got free stuff from the Americans. We would stand at Blundell Sands and there would be the American boats coming in and we would all wave and cheer. They would see us and throw stuff overboard, wrapped in cellophane. We would wait for the tide to bring them in, then all rush. Things like chewing gum, chocolates and sweets. In the streets, if the US convoys were coming through, going to Burtonwood, we would stand by the road and they would throw things to us. The Yanks seemed to have all the stuff we didn't.'

At home, the abuse continued, with Jean's step-mother hitting her for any misdemeanour. One day when she was about seven she decided to run away to her grandmother's, though she didn't really know which was her house. 'I asked a woman in the street and she said follow me. She turned out to be my aunty. I never knew I had one. In fact, I had two.

'My gran could not put me up, as she had no room, so they went to the police as I had run away. I was taken down to Dr Barnardo's. I was checked out, forms filled in and I spent one night there. Then my gran came to see me and said that she could take me in after all. So I went to live with her again.'

Being brought up during the war, Jean didn't have things like bananas and can't remember having many biscuits either. 'Even when the war finished, we didn't have biscuits in the house very often, usually just at Easter. I did buy them now and again in shops, when you could get loose biscuits like custard creams, buying them by the pound in a paper bag. I always liked Jacob's cream crackers.

'My grandmother did all the cooking. I have no memory of my mother cooking, but then I wouldn't have, as she died when I was so young. My grandmother fed us very well – usually the same dishes on the same day of each week.

'Sunday morning we always had a cooked breakfast: egg, bacon, tomatoes – which were home-grown – black pudding and fried bread. Sunday dinner was a roast if possible, but of course during the war you couldn't always manage that. Sometimes my uncle would give us a chicken from his smallholding.

'On Monday, it would be leftovers. Tuesday and Thursday was whatever was in the cupboard.

Wednesday we would often have scouse, which was a famous Liverpool stew made from neck of lamb. Friday was fish – and on Friday we would also have tripe. Saturday lunch she cooked spare ribs or pig's feet. They were lovely, done with bread in the oven.

'My childhood memory is of eating well, but with rationing at the height of the war, perhaps we didn't eat so well as I now remember it and it must have been a struggle. But I can clearly remember all those dishes, and enjoying them. I wasn't faddy.

'I can also remember my father doing some cooking, this was after the war, when he had returned home. I never did any cooking, not when I lived at home with my grandmother. My grandmother always did her shopping at a shop called Costigan's.'

Jean loved all the wartime and post-war radio programmes, like ITMA – *It's That Man Again*, starring Tommy Handley, who came originally from Liverpool. It was mainly an adult show, with funny voices and catch phrases and some double entendres. *Dick Barton, Special Agent*, appealed mainly to younger people. It was a fifteen-minute exciting serial story which came on every evening on the BBC Light Programme at 6.45. Ex-commando Captain Dick Barton, who had a clipped posh voice, aided by Jock, who was Scottish, and Snowy, a cockney, saved the nation from baddies every evening. Children all over the country, as soon as they heard the signature tune, rushed in from playing in the street to catch the next exciting episode. It always finished on a cliff-hanger, usually with the words 'Quick, Jock, Snowy...' You then had to wait till the next day to hear what happened. It ran from 1946 to 1951 and at its height had twenty-one million listeners.

Despite all the various dramas and deprivations in her early years, Jean passed the Eleven Plus, or the 'scholarship' as it was known in Liverpool. Along with two others girls from her class she found herself at Grove Street College, a girls' grammar school. She had to have a proper uniform, complete with a velour hat in winter and a straw hat in summer, which was paid for by the Education Department, on the grounds that she was a semi-orphan.

After two years, her stepmother reappeared in her life, insisting that Jean returned home to live with her and Jean's father. By this time her father and step-mother had had a child, a boy. Jean, by then aged twelve, suspects she was being seen as cheap labour again, to be a babysitter for her half-brother.

Not long after she had returned, her stepmother said the tram fares into town to her grammar school were too expensive, so Jean had to leave school and go to the local secondary school nearby.

At fourteen, Jean fell ill. She was found to have polio, then X-rays discovered TB, which is what her mother had died of. For the next year she was in hospital at Fazackerley, in the isolation wing, then in the sanatorium, where she could have school lessons.

Aged sixteen, Jean left school and got a job in the offices of the *Liverpool Echo* in the advertising department, then moved on to work at Vernons Pools.

Vernons Pools, founded in 1925, and Littlewoods, founded in 1923, both originating in Liverpool, dominated the football pools business for decades and were deadly rivals. In 1935, Littlewoods hired a plane to fly over London with a streamer behind which read LITTLEWOODS ABOVE ALL!

By 1948, the pools companies were taking in £50 million a year in bets from eight million punters – with the government grabbing a large slice in tax. The most popular was the treble chance, where you ticked eight games, hoping they would all be score draws. The first big individual win to hit the national headlines was in 1961 when Viv Nicholson – famous for *Spend Spend Spend* – won £152,319. Ten years later, the prize had reached £500,000.

The prizes were not as enormous in the 1950s when Jean was working there, but while checking the pools one day in 1953, Jean came across eight correct draws in a row, thus winning the treble chance. When the winner was announced, he asked for a tour of Vernons. While there, he asked to meet the girl who had first spotted his winning line.

'He offered to give me something, but I refused. It would not have been correct.' As a working woman, though still a teenager, Jean was earning good money, making lots of new friends, but still her stepmother was trying to dominate her life. However, unbeknown to her stepmother she managed to arrange a holiday in North Wales with five of her girlfriends. They booked two caravans, three girls in each, and had a good time, meeting some lads from Liverpool who were also on their summer holidays. She swapped addresses with a couple of the boys.

'A few weeks later, I got home one day from work to find my stepmother in a fury. She sent me straight to my room. When my dad came home, I could hear her shouting at him as I sat on the stairs.

'She had opened a letter from one of the boys I had met. She said it showed I was going out with a married man and I was pregnant. It was totally untrue. She had read things between the lines that weren't there.

'So that determined me. I couldn't stay at home any longer. When I got my wages that Friday, I answered an advert for a bedsit, went to see it and paid two weeks ahead and moved in.

'I sat in the dark that first night and wrote a letter to my dad. I went in the dark and put the letter through his letterbox. I told him what I had done, but did not reveal my address. I said the things my stepmother has said were a pack of lies. I didn't want to see her again. Nothing had happened with those boys, not even kissing and cuddling. We just sort of socialised together. I was very young and very innocent.'

Not long afterwards while at work at Vernons, someone came round recruiting girls for the Women's Royal Auxiliary Air Force. A group joined up, including Jean. They wore uniform, went on manoeuvres, were taught various skills and also got paid. Jean became a plotter – plotting aeroplane routes. There were weekend camps, but Jean was unable to attend them because of her history of TB.

Now that she was a working and independent woman she was able to spend a bit more on clothes, but was never all that obsessed by fashion.

'My stepmother or gran bought my clothes when I was young and they were mainly second hand. As a teenager my stepmother bought me my first stockings – and they were thick rayon and they itched like anything. When I had some money I went out and bought my first pair of nylons. They had a nice silk sheen, with a nice black seam up the back.

'I had a party once, when I was living with my gran, and my aunty bought me some French knickers. I was fifteen at the time, and had just come out of hospital, so the party was a special treat. My stepmother went mad when she heard.'

French knickers, which were silky and loose, were indeed considered very naughty, not the sort of thing respectable young women were supposed to wear in the 1940s and '50s.

'I mainly did my hair myself, though I would have it cut now and again at the hairdresser. It had a natural wave. It was long when I was small but my stepmother had it cut short. One time the hairdresser cut it so short it was cut right up to my ears and my stepmother went mad.

'The music I liked when I was young was Irish songs, because my grandmother sang them. When I heard Bing Crosby, I thought he was lovely. I also liked Andy Williams and Doris Day, all those nice singers of the time. Among the film stars I liked Cary Grant, Gregory Peck, Charlton Heston. One of my heroes, you might say, I mean heroines, was Bessy Braddock, the Liverpool MP. She was such a character.

'I don't think I was ever really interested in fashion styles, though I could see that Christian Dior clothes were good but very expensive. I usually wore cardigans, blouses and skirts. I never liked trousers and never wore them.

'When I went out in the evening I used to wear a taffeta skirt in two colours – black on one side and the other side was red or green – with an underskirt underneath, made of layers of tulle.'

One day in 1955, aged nineteen, after a few drinks at the WVS club, where all the forces socialised, Jean got on the bus to go home. She went upstairs to find it was full of soldiers

'An army lad came and sat down beside me. He asked me where I was going. I said West Derby. When the conductress came round, he said, "Two to West Derby please," and bought two tickets. I thought cheeky devil, who does he think he is.'

They got off the bus together at her stop. Jean started walking towards her street, followed by the cheeky soldier, chatting away. She did not want to reveal her exact address, or that she was living alone in a bedsit, and earning a very good wage at Vernons, all of which would have made any young soldier start panting. So she stopped before she got to her house, and bid him farewell. But she did agree to meet him again.

Jack was a young soldier from Carlisle. He was in the REME, stationed in Liverpool, having signed on aged seventeen in 1953 as a regular for twenty-two years, with the option of leaving every three years. He had for a while been transferred to the 10th Royal Hussars, who were known as the Shining Tenth. 'I soon found out why. All you did was shine and polish your uniform.'

Jean and Jack went out for about a year, by which time Jack came to the end of his three-year period. There was not a great deal to hold Jean to Liverpool, having no mother and disliking her stepmother. They decided to move to Jack's hometown of Carlisle, but still as single people. Jack went back to living with his family while Jean found a bedsit in Carlisle and an office job at 14 MU.

In Carlisle, during and just after the war, thousands of people worked at 14 MU. Ivy's father worked there, and most Carlisle people knew someone at 14 MU. It was considered a cushy number, a holiday camp, partly because outsiders never really knew exactly what work was carried out there. MU stood for 'maintenance unit', supplying parts for the RAF – which could be anything from half a plane to a sheet of notepaper – hence it needed hangars and warehouses, offices and storerooms, plus an army of labourers, storemen and clerks. Carlisle's 14 MU even had thirteen miles of its own railway. It sounds a bit now like an early version of an Amazon warehouse.

There were seven MUs scattered around the UK, all classified as secret, each carrying a full range of stock just in case any of them got hit by an air raid. In 1945, the Carlisle one employed 4,300 people, 784 of them uniformed, the rest civilians, half of whom were women workers.

Jean had hardly settled into Carlisle and into her job at 14 MU when Jack was called up. He was still officially a Reservist and the REME wanted him back because of the Suez crisis. On 26 July 1956, General Nasser, the president of Egypt, had nationalised the Suez canal, much to the fury of Britain, France and Israel, who mobilised their forces and started bombing Cairo.

Jean was getting over the shock of finding Jack was going abroad, possibly to fight in a war, when she discovered she was pregnant.

'I never thought of having an abortion. There were back-street abortionists you could go into those days, but I didn't fancy it. I'm not religious, but I feel aborting is killing a human being.'

They decided they had better quickly get married, which they did on 8 September 1956, at Carlisle register office. They also managed to get a council house.

Then things began to look up. Jack was not sent to Suez after all. Instead he was stationed for several months at Cark, in the south of Cumbria. He was back home in Carlisle by Christmas, the Suez crisis now over. He then got work in Carlisle as a driver.

In April 1957 Jean went into Fusehill maternity hospital for what she thought was her normal check up, not realising how near term she was.

'The doctor examined me and said I had to stay in. I said I can't. I have to go home and make my husband's dinner. He said OK, but come straight back.'

On her return, she went into the labour ward where she gave birth to a fine bouncing boy. He was later followed by two other boys and a daughter.

It was in 1971 when her youngest was aged five and at primary school that Jean decided she wanted to go back to some sort of work. Jack was still working as a driver, but they had little money and Jack wanted a car of his own.

She applied to Carr's – even though the wages seemed to her pretty miserable, compared with her last job in Liverpool. Carr's were offering £3 a week whereas back at Vernons she had been on up to £15 a week. This had included a Christmas bonus and also a bonus for being able to set a record by sorting a thousand pools coupons in twenty-five minutes.

'But I heard Carr's was considered a good job. All the Carlisle women who worked there seemed to like it.'

Alas, she was turned down. She was interviewed by a personnel manager who looked at her CV, saw she had worked at the offices of the *Liverpool Echo* and at Vernons Pools.

'She told me I would not like factory work and could not offer me the job. That was a bit of a disappointment. We did need the extra money.'

However, she went back after a few months and pleaded for a job, asking at least for a two-week trial, to see how she got on.

And so it was agreed. In April 1971, Jean started work at Carr's. She was a Liverpool woman, not a local, now aged thirty-five with three young children, who had had no experience of work in Carlisle, or any idea of what it might be like to be a factory worker.

Chapter 8
Ivy

Ivy was still working at Carr's when Jean joined, and she was one of the old hands who helped the new girl to settle in.

For her first ten years at Carr's, Ivy had had no thought or desire for promotion. She was content to do her basic packing job.

'I used to tell the new girls, all these young slips of things, that I had been there since the factory had been built in 1837. In fact, I had walked all the way from Kendal to Carlisle with John Dodgson Carr to open his first shop in Castle Street. They believed me, of course, knowing nothing about the history of the firm.'

She was no longer as giddy and daft as when she had started, jumping and dancing around, but she had survived one mishap. It affected her job at Carr's, but in fact it was not caused at work but at the hairdresser's.

'I went to have a perm and the girl put these hot curlers on me. I had to sit for ages with them on, but somehow they slipped down and burned me ears! After a few days, my ears went funny, a sort of nasty rash down the side of my face. I went to the surgery at work to tell them, as everyone could see it by now.

'We did have a nurse at work who came round, but she wasn't much good. Whether you had a cut finger or your head had come off and you were carrying it under your arms, she would still give you an Anadin. I never knew her name, I just used to call her Nurse Anadin.

'This time I realised I had something nasty, which is why I went to the surgery. They said I had dermatitis. I was immediately taken off packing and told to go home. I went home, crying, worried about losing my job and losing my wages. I felt dirty. Anyway I was given penicillin and after a few weeks it cleared up and I came back to work.'

It was after ten years at Carr's that Ivy first found herself being asked to help with training some of the new girls, though not receiving any official promotion, or extra pay.

'I wasn't bothered about getting extra money. I just enjoyed helping the new girls. I had about eight I was to look after, mostly young girls straight from school. They were all lovely, all hard-working, and would never abuse things, like taking too long a break. If they get trained right, they wouldn't do that.

'But some of them would be in tears in the first few weeks, not being able to cope – especially when they had to do night shifts. Night shifts did not bother me. I would often swap with someone, as a favour, if they couldn't manage it, because of their boyfriend or husband or children. I was single, so it didn't make much difference to me.'

Then one day, Ivy got a real promotion.

'It was a Friday evening, end of the week, and I was just about leave when John Robinson, the manager of the bakehouse, shouted across to me. "Ivy! Pink overalls on Monday, all right?"'

That was all he said. But Ivy knew what it meant. She had become a charge hand. By now it was the early 1960s and she had been working at Carr's for almost fifteen years before the call had come.

She was still unmarried, living at home, with her mother. Ivy's father had died some time ago, in 1951 aged sixty. Her brother Tommy had got married, with Ivy as a bridesmaid, and had his own family to look after.

When her mother's health began to fail, Ivy found herself increasingly looking after her, which naturally curtailed her own social life and the chances of having a boyfriend or going away on holidays. Such has so often been the position of an unmarried daughter when a widowed mother falls ill.

'The doctors began to talk about putting her in a home, but I wasn't having any of that. No one was putting my mother away.'

So Ivy gave up work and for nine months stayed at home, looking after her mother. She died aged sixty-four in her own home, as she had always wanted. This was in the Raffles council house in Dalton Avenue where she had lived since Ivy was born. Ivy took over the rental, living there on her own.

After nine months at home, Ivy decided to go back to work at Carr's, back on the assembly line, back to being a charge hand on Rich Desserts.

However, there were some clouds hovering on the horizon which began to worry all the Carr's workers, especially with so many of them coming from the same families and therefore so dependent on employment from the same firm.

When Ivy had joined in 1948, the post-war boom was just beginning and by 1954 Carr's workforce was soon up to 2,500, almost as high as in the 1920s and '30s when it had been 3,000.

The firm was still very successful, a bright star in the biscuit firmament, but the field had become very crowded and competitive since J.D. had first opened his factory in 1837.

Throughout the nineteenth century all the biscuit makers had taken advantage of the social and economic changes, with commuter trains creating suburbs and people on trains or standing at stations enjoying a biscuit to keep themselves going. In the twentieth century, teashops spread out all over the country, where secretaries and working girls could go to for a quick snack on their own.

The rival biscuit firms competed to think of new lines, new tastes, new shapes, sending out hundreds of salesmen to get orders, spending fortunes on newspaper advertisements and promotions.

The biscuit firm that claimed to be Britain's oldest was Crawford, who could trace their origins back to a bakery shop in Edinburgh in 1813 – J.D. Carr's

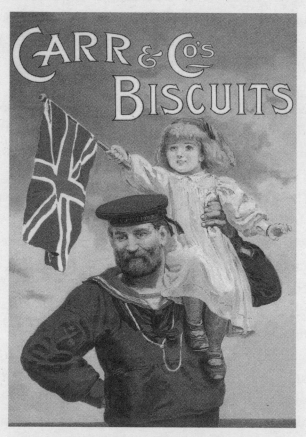

Classic Victorian advertisement for Carr's biscuits

Carlisle shop did not open till 1831. But it wasn't till the 1860s when Crawford opened a factory in Liverpool that they really expanded.

McFarlane Lang, another leading Scottish firm, originated in Glasgow in the 1840s, while the McVitie family, later McVitie's and Price, originated in Dumfries. They started up properly in business in Edinburgh in the 1830s – making their name with the patenting of digestives in 1890, so called because they contained bicarbonate of soda, which in theory helped digestion. In 1925, McVitie's went one better, creating one of the all-time favourite biscuits – chocolate digestives.

It's noticeable how many of our best-known biscuit firms, their names still recognisable today, began in Scotland. Is it because the Scots have always had a sweet tooth, or is it because the tradition of baking scones, shortbread and oatcakes had been passed on through the generations, long before factories began?

By the end of the nineteenth century, the world's biggest biscuit makers had become Huntley & Palmers, whose origins date back to 1822. Like the Carr's, they were Quakers and like J.D. Carr, Joseph Huntley had begun as a baker. His bakery shop was just one of thirty in Reading at the time, but it happened to be located on the main London road, opposite the main posting inn for the stage coaches to London, Bristol, Bath and the West Country. He found passengers were buying cakes and biscuits from him to eat on the journey, as the refreshment prices in the posting inn itself were so expensive. He started sending his delivery boy with a basket of biscuits to sell to passengers as they waited in the inn yard while the horses were changed. By supplying the carriage trade, his biscuits therefore had a wider sale and popularity than would normally have been the case.

Joseph then fell ill, but he was joined by a cousin, also a Quaker, George Palmer, and the firm became Huntley & Palmers. They built their Reading factory in 1846, by which time they were putting their biscuits into tins, making them last longer on the coach journey. By 1900 they were employing 5,000 people and claimed to be the world's biggest biscuit factory. Reading became known as the biscuit town and their football team, Reading FC, were known for many years as the Biscuitmen. (Today, they tend to be known as the Royals, after the Royal County of Berkshire.)

By the 1930s, Meredith & Drew in London – founded by another baker, William Meredith, in the 1830s – had begun to claim the top spot, boasting they were now Britain's biggest biscuit makers. In their advertising, they said they used only the finest eggs – from their own hens in Jersey – and only used Irish or French butter. They got their Royal Warrant in 1902 and, like Carr's and all the other leading manufacturers, they were quick to help out in national emergencies, knowing it would reflect well on them. One of Meredith & Drew's prize possessions was a handwritten letter from Lord Kitchener, thanking them for a gift of biscuits to the troops.

Most of our leading biscuit firms always seemed to think up something from their past or present that they could boast about in their advertising. All part of the war between them and the battle for our custom.

In 1921 the first of some major reorganising took place when Huntley & Palmers and Peek Frean in London combined to call themselves Associated Biscuit Manufacturers. Peek Frean was the firm that owed a lot of its success to John Carr, the much younger brother of J.D.

In 1948 came another important joining together when the two big Scottish firms, McVitie's and Crawford's, combined to form United Biscuits.

Carr's meanwhile, still being run by the descendants of J.D. Carr, remained an independent company. They had, of course, their own proud boast, which their rivals agreed was pretty well true: THE BIRTH-PLACE OF THE BISCUIT INDUSTRY. The slogan appeared on the main walls of the front of the Carlisle factory and also on their advertising, no doubt bringing a small glow of pride to Ivy and all the other faithful workers.

When Ivy and Dulcie first joined – in 1948 and in 1954 – the Carr family were still firmly in control, and still took a personal interest as their forefathers had done, cheering on the workers, appealing to their loyalty. One of the bonding elements in the Carr's factory family of workers, which helped to keep them all together and be inspired by the firm's heritage and its present-day successes, was the Carr's staff magazine, the *Topper Off*.

It began in 1928, the idea of the formidable Miss Nora Wynn, who was appointed Lady Superintendent by Theodore Carr in 1920. She was in effect the personnel manager, looking after the welfare of all the women, both their physical and mental well-being. The title, the *Topper Off*, referred to the girl who finally inspected the contents of a tin before the lid went on.

'The next time that lid is removed,' said an editorial in the first edition, explaining the title, 'it is by the customer, who will judge Carr's of Carlisle by what meets his eye. So in our magazine. The things that go into the life of a factory such as ours are infinite; they go to make up the life and character of a community.'

The magazine was a moral lifter, hurrah for us and our happy, cheerful staff, which gave reports on all the clubs and staff events and listed the international prizes for biscuits that the company had won in Paris, Berlin and Amsterdam. The message was clear: the workers should be proud of their firm, still family run, which cared for the welfare of all its staff and even in hard times, it was still doing well.

The early issues, in 1928–29, included some unusual features, such as an article about the women workers at a rubber goods factory in China and an article on Kenya by Allen Carr. There were reports on the football and hockey clubs, both with their own pitches at Carr's own sports field on Newtown Road. The 1928 staff dinner, presumably for the office staff, not the humble production-line workers, was held at the Crown and Mitre, Carlisle's top hotel.

There were also some jokes. One of them was about a man who had just married the daughter of a wealthy biscuit maker. A friend meets him in the street and congratulates him. 'You've taken not just the cake but the biscuit,' says his friend. 'Yes,' the man replies. 'And the dough with it.'

The use here of dough meaning money, a nineteenth-century American phrase, is interesting. It is often thought to have become popular only during the Second World War, brought over by the American troops, but clearly it had reached Carlisle by the 1920s.

The first nine issues of *Topper Off*, twenty-four pages each, featured on the cover a Lake District or rural scene, and no sign of any ugly factory buildings. For its tenth issue, Christmas 1929, the front cover is devoted to a handwritten letter from Theodore Carr, grandson of J.D., and now chairman. He sends festive wishes and signs off 'Heartiest greetings, your friend and chairman'. How many chairmen these days look upon themselves as a friend of the workers?

In 1948, when Ivy joined, the magazine was up to forty pages. There were a lot more contributions from ordinary workers and also a column by someone calling themselves 'Airtight' who thanks the girls for all their Valentines and gives them advice about going on their holidays. 'Beware of strange young men with large moustachios and one glass eye. Never accept a cigar from them.' Girls – whether packers or office staff – were going no further than Silloth or Blackpool in 1948, if they were lucky, and were pretty unlikely to smoke cigars, so the warning seems rather redundant.

A women's column advises always to use curlers at night. To look neat and tidy you could not beat 'our old friends TIME and THOUGHT'. There were hints on how to make the most of your coupons – particularly your clothing coupons – for rationing continued in the UK till well into the 1950s.

A most informative article explained the history of the matzos, and their religious significance. During the recent war, a matzo warehouse in London had been bombed but Carr's had increased production to help the Jewish population, of which it said there were currently 400,000 in the UK.

There were lots of retirements, with several women having achieved forty-five years of service, which doubtless fifteen-year-old Ivy scoffed at when she read about them in the *Topper Off*, wondering how anyone could possibly stay that long.

There was a list of recent weddings in the autumn issue 1948, giving the names of twenty-two Carr's female workers and the men they had married. Did Ivy wonder if one day she would be one of them?

Sixteen years later, in February 1964, by which time Ivy was a charge hand, the *Topper Off* had become a bumper production of sixty-four pages, glossy with lots of pictures and a colour cover. It listed all the recent achievements, such as providing Carr's Water Biscuits for a packed luncheon of 5,000 directors at the Albert Hall and being displayed on a stall at the Confectionery Exposition in Paris. There were several pages of overseas news, featuring Carr's sales forces and agents all round the world, including Turkey, the Canary Islands, Denmark, Sweden and Paris.

At home, the success of Carr's Golf Club against Hudson Scott Tin Box Factory is highlighted – the team includes members of the Carr family. The bowls club had been to play in Sunderland at the Pyrex sports stadium. The gardening club was thriving and there was a works library, available to all, which contained 350 books.

Allen Carr is photographed giving out gold watches for long service, seven ladies having achieved more than forty years. There were two pages of recent marriages – twenty-five women workers having got married. Most of them seemed to be working in the chocolate department. None of the bridegrooms' jobs are listed, which indicates the woman had married out, i.e., to non-Carr's workers – the days of internal romances, which Eric Wallace had enjoyed, perhaps being fewer or perhaps more discreet.

A detailed account of how the wages department operated reveals there were 1,300 workers in 1964, so numbers had dropped since the 1950s. They were using thirty-four different clocks for clocking in. Piece-work was still being done.

There were two unusual features, which one might not have expected in a works magazine. A long article by the export manager recounts his meeting in Germany 1945 with Dr Konrad Adenauer, later the German chancellor, then leader of the Catholic Democrat Party in Westphalia.

Equally historic, at least in the realms of pop music history, is a first-person description of the Beatles concert at the Lonsdale cinema in Carlisle on 21 November 1963. First-hand printed reports of a Beatles concert by a young fan were unusual at this stage, but she is not named. Presumably it was one of the younger cracker packers on her evening off.

That handsome, fun-filled, fact-packed issue of the *Topper Off* which appeared in February 1964 is therefore not just of interest to Carr's staff and biscuit historians but with the Adenauer story and the early Beatles concert it covered by chance some interesting political and social events of the day.

Alas, it also turned out to be the last issue of *Topper Off*. They were not aware of it, or at least there is no editorial reference in the magazine to the dramatic event that happened in early 1964.

Carr's of Carlisle had been taken over. The family had sold out their remaining shares and given up the reins, which had been handed down through the generations since Jonathan Dodgson Carr began it all in 1831.

The big bad wolf who had appeared and gobbled them up was not a rival biscuit firm, which might have been expected, but a financial entrepreneur and maverick gobbler up of companies – Jimmy Goldsmith. His company Cavenham Foods was now the new owner of Carr's of Carlisle.

His fantasy, so it appeared to the business community at the time, was to buy as many biscuit companies as he could. According to Ian Carr, who was one of the Carr's directors at the time, Goldsmith wanted to buy Associated Biscuits, which comprised Huntley & Palmers, Peek Frean and Jacob's. He would then have only United Biscuits, the other main group, to contend with.

Goldsmith was of Anglo-French origin, born in 1933, educated at Eton, a gambler and womaniser, who ran off at the age of twenty with a seventeen-year-old Bolivian tin heiress. He ended up getting married three times. 'When a man marries his mistress, he creates a vacancy,' so he famously said. His children include Zak Goldsmith, the Tory MP, and Jemima Khan, the writer and socialite.

From the 1960s onwards, Jimmy Goldsmith was voraciously buying up companies in the food business, including Bovril, immediately selling off their South American interests. He was feared as an asset stripper, who had no real interest or knowledge of the food business, least of all biscuits, but the Carr's board, worried about rising costs and narrower margins, decided to sell when Mr Goldsmith made a handsome cash offer for all the shares.

It marked the end of the Carr family connection with Carr's biscuits. Carr's Flour Mills, still going strong, which J.D. himself had set up, had split from the biscuit factory back in 1908 and become an independent company, though still, in 1964, with members of the Carr family on the board and holding minority shares.

Mr Goldsmith promised that he would keep Carr's of Carlisle in full operation. Which not everyone believed.

Chapter 9
Jean

When Jean, who had grown up in Liverpool, married a Carlisle soldier and had come to live in the town, started at Carr's in April 1971, Jimmy Goldsmith and Cavenham Foods had been running the factory for seven years.

Despite the fears and rumours, no closures had taken place, nothing much had changed and things ticked over much as they had done in 1964. Workers and local people still called it Carr's and the name still appeared on their famous water biscuits.

Until she came to Carlisle, Jean had never heard of Carr's. In Liverpool the two biscuit factories everyone had heard of were Crawford's and Jacob's, where many of her friends worked. Crawford's, the one that called itself the world's oldest biscuit maker, had opened a Liverpool factory in 1860. Jacob's, originally from Ireland, had opened their Liverpool factory in 1914.

Jean's first impression of Carr's was of a lovely smell – and also the noise, but she doesn't remember being overwhelmed by the size of the factory, like most Carlisle born-and-bred workers. She had worked in large establishments before, with lots of people, though never in a factory with machinery, hence being struck by the noise.

'I don't remember getting lost. We were shown around for the first few days till you got used to the place.'

Jean's first job at Carr's was on Lifeboat biscuits, standing at a bench with six other girls, taking the biscuits out of a very big tin and putting twelve at a time into a smaller tin, then closing the lid.

'If you didn't cut your fingers on the tins then you cut them on the paper packing. The biscuits were thick and hard as rock.'

There was no conveyor belt bringing the Lifeboat biscuits in or out. Barrowmen and barrow boys were still bringing in the big tins filled with biscuits and taking away the little tins.

Jean was then moved on to what was known as D Line, where shortcake biscuits did come on a conveyor belt, direct from the oven, before being packed in tins. Eight girls, plus a charge hand, stood either side of the belt and changed places at intervals to give their shoulders and arms a rest. One of them always had to keep an eye on the biscuits in case they fell off, as the conveyor belt was on a slope from the ovens. There was also one man working in their team, or at least assisting, a machine operator who made sure the belt was operating properly.

Jean had chosen to work the evening shift, from six to ten, as her three children were still quite young, aged from five to fourteen. Her husband Jack, after a day lorry driving, looked after them when he came home.

'As he came in, I left, leaving his tea ready for him. For the next eleven years I hardly saw him, except at weekends.'

By the time Jean started, the workers were not allowed to take their overalls out of the factory at all, which was what Ivy had done. It was feared they might pick up nasty infections from the street or buses or in their own homes. Instead, each was given their own locker at work. The factory was now doing the washing. When she started, the overalls – as they always called them, though in fact they were more like a long house-coat, buttons at the front, down to the knees – had been made of nylon, but very soon they were upgraded to linen, which the girls liked much better.

After a year working at Carr's, Jean began to hear rumours of a takeover, or merger, something dramatic was said to be in the offing. All the other girls told her about the fears they had had eight years earlier when Cavenham had arrived out of the blue, and how it had been so sudden. Their worries came mainly afterwards, wondering what it all meant, if some workers would be laid off, but in the end, things had settled down.

Now there were rumours of another takeover, which might well turn out to be more dramatic than the last one.

'The main worry of course was that we would be closed and all put out of work, but luckily it didn't happen. In fact I have a memory that we were given a bonus, from Cavenham presumably, because they had made a good profit on the sale.'

The new owners were United Biscuits, who took over in 1972. They had closed several factories, mainly in Scotland, but at least they were long experienced in the biscuit world and had by now built a large portfolio of well-known biscuit companies, including McVitie's, McFarlane Lang, Crawford's, McDonald's, Kemps and also KP Nuts. Around the time of the Carr's takeover, United Biscuits were employing 25,000 workers, with biscuit factories in London, Liverpool. Manchester, Glasgow, Ashby de la Zouch, Halifax, Aberdeenshire, Grimsby and now Carlisle. They were turning over £150 million a year and operating in eight countries, aside from the UK.

Life and work at Carr's continued as before, with most locals and workers still calling the factory and the biscuits by their old name, even though the McVitie's sign soon started to appear on the factory walls, along with the name Carr's, and the proud boast that it was the birthplace of biscuits.

'We were told Carr's was kept going because the Table Water Biscuits were so successful. They couldn't be made anywhere else because of the water we used.

I don't know whether that was true or not, but we believed it.'

Another theory was that the good industrial relations at Carr's, with no strikes in recent decades, had been the deciding factor in keeping the Carr's factory working. But the main reason was probably simple finances – the factory was running at a profit, the site was organised and big enough to expand when needed, so why close it?

After ten years working at Carr's, Jean applied to be a charge hand. She had heard there was a vacancy and it would mean £1 more a week. She was interviewed but turned down. 'It was given to a girl who had been at Carr's longer than me. A year later, I applied again and this time got it. I then discovered I could have had it first time. They had made a mistake – she had not been there longer.'

When Jean became a charge hand, promoted to the pink overall, she managed at the same time to change her hours, moving to an early morning shift, from six in the morning till two in the afternoon.

As a charge hand, she organised the break times for the other girls, kept a list of the work done by each girl, how much had been packed, and also kept an eye out for any faults or problems with the biscuits.

'I was on Table Water for a long time and you had to make sure the edges were not burned. If that started happening, you didn't pack them, just let them continue on the belt and they fell off into a bin. If it was happening a lot, you would go and tell the foreman in charge of the oven, show him the burned ones. He would eff and blind, curse you right, left and centre.

'When I first started at Carr's, I went there and back on the bus each day, but when I went on to the morning shift, six to two, I had to start very early in the morning, so I shared a taxi with four other girls. It was quite expensive, but saved us a lot of time on very dark, cold mornings and was a lot nicer.

'But I still got the bus home at two, at the end of my shift. That was always a mad rush, with so many people clocking off at the same time. You had to queue and fight to get on the bus, so often I would just walk into town, do some shopping, and then get the bus home from the town hall. Not on a Friday, though, the centre of Carlisle was always pandemonium on a Friday – and of course even worse on a Saturday, with all the country people coming in. It still is.'

By the time Jean became a charge hand, the grade of supervisor – one rung up from charge hand – had been abolished. Next up in the hierarchy was the manager class, but she rarely saw any managers.

On the morning shift, her girls were allowed a ten-minute tea break around 7.45. If times were slack, as in winter, they might all go together, otherwise they went in relays. It had been agreed with the union that charge hands could decide the order. At eleven o'clock they had breakfast, for which they were allowed thirty minutes. Then there was another tea break around 1 p.m. of ten minutes. The welcoming hooter for the end of their shift sounded loud and clear at two o'clock.

'I never got away exactly at two, more like 2.15 as each charge hand had to show her notes to the next charge hand and tell her what had happened on that shift.'

Being on the Table Water room, which was downstairs, was probably her favourite, as it was cooler. Working upstairs always seemed to be hotter.

'The one I didn't like was the cheese biscuits. This was upstairs and we only had a half wall dividing us from the bakehouse ovens – so all the heat rose up. They did provide us with fans, and also lemonade with ice in buckets. But it was still awful, over 80 degrees. You sweated for the whole shift.'

Despite the tropical heat of the cheese biscuits, she found the noise bearable. In fact she can't remember any of the workplaces she worked in where the noise of machines totally drowned out conversations. Even in the noisiest places, they always managed to chatter away while working.

'That's what I liked best about the job – talking to the lasses. We never stopped. That's what you did all day long. Sometimes of course you had to shout to be heard.'

The chat was rarely anything intimate or confessional, but general family talk, about boyfriends or husbands, going over the scraps of their ordinary family life, children, clothes, TV programmes, holidays.

Jean had passed the Eleven Plus and for two years in Liverpool had been at a grammar school, but not for a moment did she feel intellectually superior or that the repetitive work of packing biscuits was beneath her.

'It didn't bother me, the actual work. I was never bored. The pleasure was in that chat with the lasses. That kept me going every day. When I became a charge hand, I liked the minor responsibility.

'I suppose I could have had an office job, but it was too late for that really when I joined Carr's, not at my age. Anyway, I was proud of Carr's and proud of being a charge hand.'

What she did not enjoy quite as much as she had hoped was Carlisle itself. Coming from Liverpool she had found some cultural and economic shocks.

'Almost the first day I arrived in 1955 I was walking down Botchergate with Jack and we came to Timpson's, the shoe shop, same as the one we had in Liverpool.

'I was looking in the window and I realised a pair in the window was the same pair as I had on that day, which I had bought in Timpson's in Liverpool just a week earlier. The price in the window was twenty-one shillings eleven pence – yet I had paid only nineteen shillings eleven pence in Liverpool for exactly the same shoes.

'I turned to Jack and said, "Look at that, how do you live in this damn city with prices like that?" He wasn't aware of the difference.

'Then I began to notice that all foods and clothes were more expensive than in Liverpool. Jack had no idea what I was on about. Or any interest. It was just normal to him.

'It's still much the same – ordinary things in Carlisle are more expensive than Liverpool. And new fashions didn't come as quickly into the Carlisle shops.

'I used to think it was because of the transport. You know, we had the docks in Liverpool while here things had to come all the way by lorry, which put up the prices. But I don't think it's that. I think it's probably more like lack of competition. We had loads of supermarkets in Liverpool, cheap ones and expensive ones, long before Carlisle. For a long time Carlisle only had Marks & Spencer, which is not cheap. They have more supermarkets now, but still don't have many cheap shops or stalls, not like Liverpool.

'I honestly don't know how many of the ordinary working people in Carlisle survive. The wages are still lower here than elsewhere, yet prices are higher. I realised that the day I started at Carr's on £3 a week, compared with £15 at Vernons. I know that was because I very good at my job and got bonuses, but even so, ordinary jobs in Liverpool, like packing biscuits at Crawford's, were paid better than doing the same sort of thing at Carr's.'

So perhaps that was another reason why Carr's survived during the two takeovers – cheaper labour.

Jean also missed the theatres, dance halls, clubs and cinemas of Liverpool. Carlisle's only theatre Her Majesty's, where once Charlie Chaplin had performed, closed in 1963. It was turned into a bingo hall then demolished in 1979 to make way for a car park. By the 1980s, there were half as many cinemas as there had been when Ivy was a girl.

'Something else I noticed in the 1950s when I first arrived – the lack of Teddy boys. In Liverpool they were everywhere. They looked frightening but they weren't really.

'When Jack and I were first courting in Liverpool, we saw this group of Teddy boys in their tight trousers at a street corner. I shouted over to them, "Did your mother pour you into them or did she sew you in?" Jack took my hand and said, "Be careful, they might knock you one." I said, "Don't be daft. I know them. I went to school with some of them."

'"We won't touch her," said the leader of the Teds, "but if you touch her, we'll touch you."'

Jean was also struck by an apparent lack of friendliness and openness among Carlisle folks, as opposed to the normal Scouser.

'In my neighbourhood in West Derby, all the doors seemed to be open all the time. If I went to visit a friend, I could go straight in. The locals here seemed stand-offish, closed in, as if they don't want to be friendly. I have of course made some very good friends, and still have them, but generally I'd say the locals are not very forthcoming. They keep themselves to themselves. I don't know why.

'Even a few miles out, they seem friendlier. For example, last week I had to go for physio at Wigton, instead of the Carlisle hospital, and immediately they all called me by my first name. They never did that at the Carlisle hospital.'

Other visitors to Carlisle over the centuries have commented on the outward suspiciousness and buttoned-up nature of many of the natives – which has often been put down to Carlisle's history, being a Border town, living in fear of the Scots or the Border Reivers arriving, so best stay indoors, give nothing away, say nowt.

Even the locals have been aware of it. In a Carlisle newspaper, the *Citizen*, on 14 May 1830, there was a very cynical, scathing description of the local character.

The natives of Carlisle are neither English, Scottish nor Irish but a mongrel breed betwixt the three. They are possessed of low cunning but are often outwitted. They pride themselves on their feats of deception and will chuckle over the misfortunes of a person they may have been principally instrumental in bringing to ruin.

There was something else Jean was immediately aware of when she first arrived in Carlisle.

'I noticed straight away the lack of coloured people – and you still don't see many. At school in Liverpool, my best friend was coloured and there were others in my class. They were pure Scousers who just happened to be descendants of the African slaves who had been dumped in Liverpool. We also had a lot of Chinese. No one bothered. They were just like us really. But here in Carlisle, they have never been used to outsiders.

'I once had words at the school gate with a woman. Something silly, saying my son had done something which he hadn't. She turned round and said, "You want to go back where you come from – you foreigner!" The funny thing was she was Scottish. I said it's you who should go back to Scotland. Carlisle is in England, haven't you noticed.'

Perhaps it had been Jean's Scouse accent that had initially put local people off? She doesn't think so.

'Actually I never had a strong Liverpool accent. When I was at school in the 1940s, at the secondary not the grammar, we had elocution lessons to tone down our Scouse accents. Yes, that was surprising.

'But it is true that when I first arrived I couldn't understand them – just as much I'm sure as they couldn't understand me.'

Chapter 10
Dulcie

In 1974, when Dulcie returned to work at Carr's, after two marriages and two daughters, United Biscuits were the new owners. The Carrs had all gone, including Allen Carr, the one she had good-morninged in her earlier period as a messenger girl in the 1950s.

Dulcie was joined at Carr's by her profoundly deaf daughter Louise – making her the third generation of the females in her family to work on the lines at Carr's. Her years at the special boarding school had helped her with reading and writing and sign language, but talking was difficult.

One day, Dulcie was told that Louise was having a spot of bother. While packing biscuits, a woman working alongside Louise had upset her and had her in tears.

'She had apparently complained about Louise. "I dunno what she's on about, she can't talk properly." She was an older woman as well, someone you would have thought would have known better. But you always have one or two of these people everywhere. It's ignorance, really.'

Dulcie arrived and when she heard what had happened gave the woman a piece of her mind, which resulted in a heated argument.

'I didn't hit her. All that happened was that her face walked on to my fist...'

They were both sent home and in the subsequent investigation Dulcie was decreed to have been in the wrong, which she accepted. Dulcie and the woman were separated and she and Louise were ordered home, to await an investigation.

'We then got called to this office which seemed to be full of people. There was the personnel manager, several plant managers and a union rep. We told them what had happened, gave our side of the story, and they all listened and asked a few questions. It was pretty frightening, as we stood there in front of them all.

'The upshot was that Louise was suspended for a week and I was given a final warning about my behaviour. We were then both marched out of the office, out of the factory and escorted off the premises. I did laugh at that. It was funny because it was so out of proportion to our crime.

'As we walked out, one of the managers said to me, "Your daughter is lucky to have a job at all." Meaning, because she was deaf. That made me really mad. "And you'll be lucky if you have a job after I've reported you..." so I told him.

'But I never did. I meant to, but didn't. With hindsight, I should have done. There should have been a deaf interpreter there. Otherwise how could they have properly heard Louise's side of the story?

'Even now I wished I had lodged a formal complaint. But at the time I just accepted that we had both been wrong to get into a fight.'

Another time, Louise herself got into a squabble with another girl in front of one of the management, not a wise thing to do. Dulcie arrived to help out, and translate what Louise was trying to say, but it was too late. A certain amount of pushing had taken place between Louise and the other girl.

'Me and Louise were escorted off the premises like petty criminals. She got suspended but I didn't, as I had done nothing.'

Dulcie admits there was a time in her life when she did a lot of swearing, living up to the image of how many assume, quite wrongly of course, that women factory workers generally talk and behave.

'There were girls who did swear – because they wanted to sound big. So if you answered them back the same way that took them by surprise. I could sometimes sound like a fishwife. Bob [her husband] used to say that I must have fallen off a potter's cart. I would do much better in life if I stopped swearing. But I didn't do it all the time. Only in arguments. But swearing is part of the rich tapestry of life. Even more so now...'

In Carlisle slang, 'potters' refers to tinkers, rag-and-bone men, or anyone assumed to be part of the great uneducated, the great unwashed, most of whom traditionally had lived in the slums of Caldewgate, near the factory.

Dulcie's occasional use of swear words doesn't seem to have held her back much, being of a cheerful, outgoing disposition. It also helped that back in the seventies, many of the bosses had started like her, on the line, or as barrow boys. She had known them growing up, and they knew her.

But once reorganisation in the biscuit industry took place, and Carr's became part of a group, with sales and finance and other departments being controlled from the group's headquarters in London, more management suits arrived from outside, not all of them aware of the character of Carlisle, or its workers, or of Carr's history, manners and mores.

However, Dulcie, despite her colourful tongue, got promoted. She was given a post as timekeeper, along with another girl. There was no more money, but it was in theory a pleasanter, less physical job. It meant a bit of paperwork, keeping a record of what was happening and what was being produced on each shift. She had learned typing at the Margaret Sewell School, so office practices were not a mystery to her.

'For about three months or so I was timekeeper in

the Jews. That's what we called the department that made the Passover food, which had to be specially supervised by the rabbis. They were there all the time, during all the shifts, with their big beards and tall hats. They usually came up from Manchester, as I don't think we even had rabbis in Carlisle, not that I ever heard of. They were all very pleasant, but they did keep a very sharp eye on everything. You had to be on top of your work. Their job was to check every process and every ingredient was in accordance with Jewish law. In the Jews, they used only the best stuff.'

The history of the Jewish connection goes back to the early twentieth century and was another of Theodore Carr's initiatives. (It was during Theodore's reign that Carr's Flour Mills had been separated from the biscuits works, for complicated financial and legal reasons.)

In 1910, Theodore organised the purchase of Rakusen Brothers of London who made kosher biscuits and Passover cakes – or matzos, are they are more commonly called. A new company, Bonn & Co, was created to run the kosher business, with Theodore as chairman. The Jewish ecclesiastical establishment were concerned at first that a Gentile-owned firm could be entrusted with the task of making sure all the ingredients and the process was correct, but they were soon won over. Regular inspections had to be made, to ensure the flour was unleavened and all the ingredients kept separate from Carr's other lines, but it turned out a big success.

Over the next few decades, as can be seen from the pages of the *Topper Off*, chief rabbis were regularly photographed visiting from other countries, inspecting the process and blessing the biscuits and the workers.

The kosher work was seasonal, with a big push every New Year to get production ready for Passover in April, around Easter time.

In the tape-recorded, oral archives of Carr's workers from the past there are countless mentions of the Jews room, which clearly fascinated the Carlisle workers, not being used to Jewish people or customs.

A Miss Raven, born in 1905, who joined Carr's aged fourteen in 1919, talked about her memories of the Jews room just after the First World War – revealing that there actually was a Mr Bonn, who was nominally in charge of the firm, though it was owned by Carr's:

'Folks look at the biscuits and think it's just flour and water, but they don't know all that goes on behind it. First of all the seeds of the corn, the wheat for making the flour, that is blessed, they are very keen on blessing it, kosher they call it. The wheat is put into very clean bags and taken to the flourmills. Have you been to see the flourmills? You ought to, it's very interesting. There hasn't to be a particle of dust anywhere. They would go round with a microscope. It had to be cooked to the very second of the Jewish law and if it was a second over, the *shomerine* or overseer would discard it.

'The rabbis stayed at the Crown and Mitre hotel when they came to Carlisle. Mr Bonn saw to their catering. The ovens and the pans had to be checked so they wouldn't touch anything that had been touched by Gentiles. Later they used to have their food in the overseer's house. They wouldn't partake of any food in a Gentile's house. Mind you, the Jewish food is very good. Mr Bonn used to bring us some and it was very good.

'The chief rabbi of Ireland came over one year and he was very charming, educated at either Oxford or Cambridge, I can't remember which. He used to talk to us while he was waiting for his boat to go back over to Ireland. He ended up being the first chief rabbi of Palestine, so I was told...'

According to Miss Raven, and others who worked on the kosher biscuits in the pre-war years, the rabbi in charge, watching the process, would jangle a pocket full of half-crowns and if the production was ready on time, or even earlier, and all was correct, he would present the charge hand with half a crown, to share among the girls.

Dulcie has no memory, alas, of ever being given a half-crown during her spell in the Jews room, but she did enjoy it there and found it most interesting.

After a couple of years as a timekeeper, it was decided that two timekeepers were not strictly necessary and that one was enough. Dulcie was moved back to packing.

Dulcie returned to the line, working on Bourbon biscuits, still one of the most popular biscuits today, a best-seller in all supermarkets. They are the ones with the chocolate fondant filling sandwiched between two oblong dark biscuits. Genuine ones have the word Bourbon embossed on them and have two lines of five holes, for reasons too mysterious to fathom.

They were another of the inspired creations by Peek Frean – who had given the world the Garibaldi biscuit in 1861. Bourbons, originally called Creola, were launched in 1910 and named after the French-European royal dynasty, thus conveying an air of class and distinction. John Carr – J.D.'s younger brother – did not die till 1912, so possibly he had a hand in the creation of the Bourbons as well as the Garibaldis.

Dulcie was also on custard creams, which originated around the same period, just before the First World War. They have remained a particularly British delight, not quite as known or as scoffed abroad. Like the Bourbon, it is a sandwich, with white cream between two rectangularish biscuits. It is decorated with an elaborate baroque design, which looks equally mysterious at first, but if you study it carefully you can see it is in fact a fern motive.

Names do seem to help in the success and popularity of certain biscuits. Iced Gems, for example, sound enticing – and have been enticing biscuit lovers for over a hundred years. The gem part goes back to the 1850s and refers to the fact that they were small, little gems of biscuits, but they happened partly by accident. Mr Huntley, of Huntley & Palmers, was trying out some new recipes and the results were coming out shrunk. He liked them all the same, and decided to christen them Gems. The iced part came a few decades later, when icing machines – one of Theodore's contributions – were established in all the main biscuit factories.

Ginger nuts are spicy biscuits, with a long history, though the strength of the spice can vary. The best known and most popular today are those produced by McVitie's. It is not clear if the nut part came from the description of a red-haired person being a ginger nut – or the other way round, that red-haired people

Carr's girls at work icing biscuits in the 1920s

got so called after the success of the ginger nut. Hob Nobs and Jammy Dodgers, both excellent names, are more recent British creations. McVitie's introduced the Hob Nobs in the 1980s, a crunchy oaty biscuit with a knobbly surface. 'One nibble and you're nobbled' was an early slogan. It's now a modern classic – and you wonder how it took so long to get invented.

Jammy Dodgers go back to the 1960s and were created by the Burton biscuit company in South Wales. They are a shortbread biscuit with a jam filling, which you can just peek at through a heart-shaped hole. The name is supposed to have come from the Roger the Dodger character in the *Beano* comic. The heart-shaped hole conjures up images of the Queen of Hearts, the one who baked the tarts, which the Knave of Hearts, i.e., the Jammy Dodger, stole away. Jammy Dodgers are regularly voted the most popular biscuit among children.

Dulcie, once she had been moved on from Bourbons, found herself for a long time on assortments, a complicated process that necessitated careful packing into tins.

'The first girl on the line would put in lining paper at the bottom of the tin, then each of us would be on a different biscuit, milk chocolate digestives, custard creams or whatever. We would each add ours to the tin, then the last girl would close the tin and seal it. Rover Assortment, that was the name on the tin.

'I enjoyed it. They were all nice girls I was working with. Factory girls do have a poor name, but they come in all sorts – like a biscuit assortment. You do get every type, which outsiders don't realise. Just a few of them swear...'

One day, a manager whom she had known as a barrow boy told her there was a vacancy for a clerk – why didn't she apply? By then she had worked for almost twenty years on many different production lines. So she applied and got the job.

'I was in a little office, beside the bakery. There were five of us in the office, all women, a woman manager in charge and four of us clerks. We had to keep the records of who was working on each line, their hours and if people were off sick to move people around. We each looked after a different department. I was on assorted packing. Then there was the chocolate, the bakehouse and I've forgotten the other one.

'We each had a computer, a very early one I suppose it was, can't remember what sort now, but it was more than just a typewriter. I did know how to use a keyboard, so it wasn't too hard to pick it up.

'The girls were fine. They didn't look down on me because I had come off the line. We all sat at a desk, so it wasn't as hard as standing packing, but we still had to wear the usual white uniform. We had a white cap as well, but we didn't need to wear that when we were typing, only if we went through the bakehouse. For hygiene reasons.

'Then I seemed to lose interest after a while. It was quite demanding work. It wasn't like being on the line where you had no responsibilities at all. It was a bit stressful. I missed working on the line.'

So, after two years as a clerk in the office, Dulcie returned to the production line. She then began to be troubled by aches and pains in her legs and arms, which many of the packers on the lines have suffered from during the last 150 years or so.

'By then I'd done over twenty years at Carr's and the work was suddenly becoming so hard. I was getting sore shoulders and neck and for a time I wore a collar as I had spondylitis. I was also getting what we called bakehouse legs – which Louise got as well. It really just means varicose veins, but they look awful, bits sticking out of the back of your legs. Bob [her husband] had retired, as his health had become poor.'

Her daughter Louise had left Carr's by then, having got married and had two children. Elizabeth, her younger daughter, had also got married and had a child.

'I began to wonder whether it was worthwhile carrying on. Or whether it was time to pack up or do something else…'

Chapter 11
Dorothy

Dorothy, the girl from the country, brought up on a farm, started at Carr's in 1976, not long after Dulcie had returned. She was trained by Ivy for the first few weeks, who was still helping to teach a new generation of biscuit girls the tricks and tips.

Dorothy, having spent many years previously in the confectionery business, was by now aged thirty-seven, quite old compared with some of the girls who had come straight from school. She did meet quite a few woman of her own age, though, most of whom were married with children.

When first moving to Carlisle, she had gone to dances, at places like the Cameo and the County. She was quite happy living at home with her parents and quite happy, she says, with her own company. 'I did have men who asked me to go on holiday with them, but I said no. I had boyfriends, but nothing serious.'

She walked to work on the first day, found she could do it just fifteen minutes, and walked back and forward every day afterwards, thus saving money on bus fares.

Like most new workers, Dorothy was overwhelmed by the size of the factory, and all the old bits, scattered around, at the end of corridors and across yards. She often got lost in the first few weeks and had to ask someone the way to where she was supposed to be working.

Dorothy was put on Table Water Biscuits, where she had to pack twelve packets into a box and then, if they were for export, she had to pack three of the boxes into a much bigger box, which would then have thirty-six packets in each.

The water biscuits were hot, straight from the oven, but like most of the women at the time – before health and safety took over so much of working lives – she didn't wear the gloves, preferring to get used to burning her fingers.

'The first year was the worst. I was put on the six to two shift. I don't remember being offered any other shift. I just accepted it, pleased to be in work. But it meant I had to be up at five each morning to get there. That took some getting used to, after doing normal day shifts in the other jobs I had had.

'When I got home at 2.30, I felt so tired. I would have a rest, then get up and have a cup of tea and a wash. It felt a bit funny at first, not knowing what to do with yourself for the rest of the day. But I soon settled down. I liked the six to two shift. It was no bother.

'I did dream a lot about biscuits that first year, not quite nightmares, but a bit worrying. I would dream that the biscuits were running off the band [the conveyor belt] because I had been too slow to pick them up. They were all just falling down... then I would wake up.'

She didn't find being on water biscuits all the time too boring. Dorothy manages to cope and smile and be cheerful about most things in life.

'Oh, but there was some variety. There were large water biscuits and small water biscuits and then later on we had special water biscuits which had garlic in or pepper. What was strange, when you were handling them, you couldn't smell the garlic, but everyone else in the factory would say, ooh what's that smell. When we moved away, we could smell it as well, but not when we were close up. Funny that.

'It was very hot. The forewoman would have a thermometer and when it got too hot she would make us all drink a glass of saline water. We had to drink at least one a day, to keep up our salt content, with all the sweating. You could drink more, which some lasses did. I just drank one glass a day. The saline water was kept in big buckets. Sometimes we also got given glasses of lemonade, or perhaps it was lime, which was nice. I never complained. That was just your job, how it was.

'Another funny thing, I can't remember how much I started on at Carr's – or how much I was being paid ten or twenty years later. Yet I can still remember my first wage at fifteen, straight from school: £2 7s 3d. I suppose it was because it was my first and it seemed enormous.'

On the six to two shift, most of the girls would go to the canteen for breakfast, some having a full fry-up, others just cereal, but Dorothy never did. She took her own sandwiches.

'You'll laugh at this, when I tell you my favourite sandwich was lettuce! I love lettuce. Sometimes with tomato or an egg, sometimes just lettuce. I love lettuce in the summer. And in the winter, now I think about it. I could have been a rabbit.'

She enjoyed the work, liked all the other girls, chatting to them as they packed away. While it could be noisy at times, it was never as noisy as it had been when she had worked in the textile factory as a machinist, where the machines ruined any chance of talking.

'There were a few disagreements on the water biscuits, but I would never say rows or fighting. It was usually when some lass wanted to stand at a certain place, saying she had stood there yesterday and wanted to change. I was upset by any bad language, which a few girls used all the time. It used to make me cringe.'

She pursed her lips and sucked in her breath, demonstrating how she used to react to swearing, not that it made much difference to the swearers.

She joined the union when she started at Carr's, the General Workers Union, but only because it was compulsory. When it ceased to be compulsory, she left.

'I don't really believe in unions. I know they do some good, but it seemed to me they didn't do a lot. When there were rumours of takeover bids, and we might close, I suppose they would have fought our case, but they didn't need to, as we never went on strike or closed. My dad was anti-union, so perhaps I got it from him. He had a friend, a big union man, but when he fell on hard times, they didn't help. I never knew the details, but it was a story my dad told. I always held that story against the unions.'

Unlike Dulcie, Dorothy didn't seem to suffer any physical ill-effects from all that hard work, the constant standing, constant bending, leaning backwards and forwards, plus the heat.

Most of the biscuit girls, with age, did begin to feel their backs and shoulders and legs beginning to ache, which is little wonder. It's hard to think of many other jobs in which everything is done standing up. Office workers might get backache and repetitive strains, but at least they are sitting down, taking the weight off their legs. Lorry drivers get aches, with sitting in the same position, but they have relatively comfy, well-designed seats to sit in. In jobs that require people to be on their feet all day, like shop assistants, or street sweepers, or traffic wardens, there is a chance to move around, walk somewhere, but a biscuit packer on the line is stuck, rooted to the same spot, often a very cold, concrete, uncomfortable spot, from which they had to perform unnatural, back-breaking sideways and back-wards manoeuvres.

Dorothy was one of the rare ones who never seemed to feel the physical strains. Perhaps it was with being brought up on a farm, helping with the harvests. Or perhaps it was because of her placid, laid-back temperament.

However, as the years went on, and she reached her late fifties, she was beginning to think she had had enough. She had worked twenty-two years in the same department at Carr's, as well all the years in her previous jobs.

'I had been working non-stop since I was fifteen, so that was coming up to fifty years of work all together.'

Dorothy was still unmarried, still living at home with her parents, but both were fit and well. 'I began to think that perhaps I had done my bit...'

But she decided to carry on, for a bit longer anyway. Despite beginning to find some parts of the job more tiring than she had felt earlier in her Carr's career, such as packing the tins, especially the larger, heavier ones for export, she hoped she could manage to keep going till perhaps she was sixty.

'I liked to think we were packing biscuits that were going to go all round the world. I was always quite proud of that.'

*

One of the jobs which the barrowmen and boys were there to do was hump the boxes and tins away when full, to the loading bays, but while packing them, either with packaging to protect the biscuits, or the biscuits themselves, the women had to move them around, often giving themselves some nasty cuts.

Tins had been used at Carr's from the early decades. However, it is generally accepted among biscuit historians that packing biscuits into tins probably first started in the 1840s with Huntley & Palmers of Reading. At least that is what the firm has claimed. Immediately all the rivals started doing the same, but Carr's had an advantage in having one of the most innovative tin makers right on their door step, Hudson Scott, up to date with the latest developments.

Being able to decorate the tins, by sticking on elaborately printed labels, made them more attractive, for customers and the trade. As early as 1847 Carr's was boasting about its pretty tins, according to an advertisement in the *Handbook to the Lancaster and Carlisle Railway*: 'Packed in neat tin boxes of three and five pounds, labelled with an engraving of the City of Carlisle, the Royal Arms and the maker's name.'

Biscuit tins had first come in solely to protect the biscuits, just as tins were being used to transport and protect mustard, tobacco and tea, all of them perishable goods, keeping them safe and dry over long journeys, or over a length of time. But once tins could be decorated, made to look pretty and attractive in themselves, they became an important selling tool. All sorts of other kinds of goods started to appear packed in tins, when often the use of tin was not strictly necessary – such as corsets, make-up, and even nails. A decent-looking tin, so it was thought, could make any old product desirable.

Nice, well-made biscuit tins could also be used by shopkeepers for display, and not just for transport, especially if they had a glass top or a glass side, through which the customer could peer and ogle at the tasty contents.

The big breakthrough in tin decoration came in the 1860s when direct printing on to the tins themselves became possible, thanks to new techniques and inventions. Hudson Scott, with their expertise in printing acquired before they went into tin making, established a reputation at the top end of the market, becoming known for the fine quality of their tins. They hired some well-known designers of the day, such as John Bushby, to do the art work.

Biscuit tins became works of art in their own right, especially at Christmas, when special efforts were made by all the biscuits manufacturers to create presentation tins, with fancier than usual assortments and also much fancier decorations and designs, such as the latest art nouveau styles.

And of course well-made tins were pretty useful – and not just among our brave imperial soldiers who filled them with sand to build barricades. People began to save the prettier tins, and reuse them for their own purposes, such as sewing boxes, or to store jewellery, stationery and stamps, or their precious savings.

The biscuit and tin manufacturers, ever alert to what their customers were liking and doing, then began to dream up biscuit tins which looked like something else, or were ready to be converted to a secondary purpose, once the biscuits had been consumed.

With improving techniques, they could produce much more unusual shapes and designs rather than the basic rectangular tins, in which biscuits were simply laid out. Biscuit tins that could then be used as glove boxes and handkerchief boxes were fairly obvious developments, but some were not so obvious. Such as money boxes.

Around 1900 Carr's had a biscuit tin in the shape of a money box with a handle on the top and a lid which could be locked. It was black and looked more like a small safe than a biscuit tin, and came complete with a key. They also had a biscuit tin that could double up later as a small kit bag.

Naturally, all the rival companies competed to produce unusual but desirable biscuit tins. If tins were kept after the biscuits had been consumed, on display

The women of 'Canal Block Packet Section',
taken around 1929

in your house, or carried around in your hand as a
bag, or on your back as a kit bag, you were of course a
walking advertisement for the manufacturer.

Huntley & Palmers had a biscuit tin in the shape
of a bookcase, with five pretend books lined up. You
couldn't actually do much with it, after you had eaten
the biscuits, apart from putting it on the shelf and say
look, children, a little pretend bookcase.

Children became a big market, once the manufacturers also realised that biscuit tins could be turned into
toys. If you made them in the shape of London buses
or lorries or trains, they became excellent free toys for
playing with, as long as you didn't cut yourself.

During the First World War, and the Second, biscuit tin production practically ceased, as tin was needed for other more vital purposes, but once the wars were over, fancy biscuit tins reappeared. In the 1920s, reflecting the flappers and high society, cocktail biscuits appeared. Inside the special tins were recipes for cocktails.

After the last war, in the 1950s, biscuit tins returned but were never as artistic and elaborate as they were in the Victorian age. The designs and printing were cheaper and they tended to show TV or film stars or old-fashioned rural scenes. Royal weddings, though, have always produced a flurry of special biscuit tins.

Today there is a great demand for vintage biscuit tins among collectors, even the ones that Ivy was packing back in the 1940s and 1950s. Victorian ones are especially desirable, or those from the 1920s. It is possible to trace a lot of our social and political and design history by collecting in biscuit tins.

They now command good prices, especially in the USA, though even in little local British auction houses unusual ones always get snapped up. In September 2013, a very nondescript bashed-up tin, with a badly reproduced Venetian illustration on the lid, had several collectors bidding against each other at Mitchell's auction in Cockermouth. It went for £150. The attraction was that on the bottom you could clearly see the words Carr's of Carlisle and also the name

Hudson Scott – names to savour if you happen to be a biscuit tin collector. It was thought to have dated to the 1890s.

The glass-topped tins that appeared on grocers' counters can go for several hundred pounds each. Even more expensive, up to a thousand pounds, are the large display cabinets, the ones with mahogany surrounds and shelves and glass doors. Those inscribed with Carr's of Carlisle and their Royal Warrant are particularly desirable.

Easier to find, and cheaper to buy, are little sample tins, hundreds of thousands of which were given away before the war. They contained just three or four biscuits, handed out in the street or put through selected letterboxes, as part of local promotions to encourage you to go to your local grocers to buy them. The collectible ones have of course to have the name of a well-known biscuit manufacturer or brand, usually long since gone, but fondly remembered.

One of the commonly seen sample biscuits tins today are the little red Carr's tins with CARR'S CARLISLE on the top. Around the sides it usually says Biscuits, Chocolates, Toffees or Celebrated Biscuits. The same little red tins were used for twenty years, which is why so many have survived. All of them are pretty and worth collecting. They're bargains at between £10 and £20, depending on condition.

If only our biscuit girls, the ones who started just after the war, could have salted away some of the Carr's biscuit tins they were packing back in the 1940s, 1950s and 1960s, they would have done wonders to their pension funds today.

Chapter 12
Barbara

Barbara, middle, as a schoolgirl in the 1960s

Barbara was in the next generation of Carr's biscuit girls. Unlike Ivy, Dulcie, Jean and Dorothy, all born in the 1930s, Barbara was born after the Second World War was over. By her own account, she was an excellent student, which in one way makes it unusual that she should ever have become a worker on the biscuit production line, as in the post-war decades young girls were slowly being encouraged to be more ambitious, assertive and independent.

'Oh yes, I was in the top three in the class all the way through. Maths came easy to me, and English. I wasn't so good on creative writing or imagining things, but I could spell properly and I understood grammar, which of course we were taught in those days, not quite like today.'

Barbara was born in George Street, Carlisle on 23 December 1953, a street which was indeed Georgian, but is has long since gone, swept away by the mad dash for modernisation, with ring roads and multi-storey council blocks which back in the sixties so many local authorities thought they ought to have. In George Street at the time was a medical centre and mini-hospital, which was where Barbara was born.

Barbara's father was a Geordie who was in the army doing his national service and stationed at Hadrian's Camp just outside Carlisle when he met Barbara's mother. She was from Carlisle, had gone to the Margaret Sewell School and had become a typist till she got married. After the army, her father became a lorry driver and they lived in a council house in Harraby, going on to have four children in all.

'At home, my parents used to get the *Daily Express* delivered and I think the *Mirror*. As a child, I used to get the *Dandy* and *Beano* and another I think called the *Topper*. Then when I became a teenager, I got *Jackie* magazine. As a girl I was in the Girl Guides. We used to meet in Trinity Parish Hall which was at the top of Stanhope Road.

'My mother cooked really well but generally we had good wholesome meals that were relatively cheap and easy to prepare as she also worked part-time to support us four kids and of course the household in general. We usually had cereals or porridge for breakfast. Of course, us kids had to have sugar on the Scott's porridge oats whereas my dad said it should have salt on, both probably a definite no-no today.

'In the winter after breakfast, just before we went to school, we all had a most unwelcome extra, the daily spoonful of – urrrrrgh! – cod liver oil.

'All us kids had school dinners which were usually a meat 'n' two veg type meal followed by a pudding such as a jam roly-poly or syrup sponge and of course most people's favourite – chocolate chip pudding and custard. Another school favourite was chocolate pudding with white sauce or on rare occasions chocolate custard.

'At home, we didn't have the same meal on the same day every week, except for Sundays. Sunday was different; we had a cooked breakfast, the full Monty you would say nowadays, bacon, eggs, sausage, tomato, beans, black pudding, mushrooms and fried bread or potato scones. This was followed much later in the day, maybe around 3 p.m, by a Sunday roast with all the trimmings and Yorkshire puddings with whatever the roast was, just cos we all liked them. If there was ever anything left over, even if it was just gravy, my dad would have it with a slice of bread. Teatime was maybe a sandwich and always cake and biscuits.

'On weekdays we might have shepherd's pie or mince and dumplings or good old egg 'n' chips or fish finger 'n' chips. In the summertime there were strawberries fresh from the garden and new potatoes. Dad also grew cabbages and carrots and onions and rhubarb. Mam used to bake usually once a week. Apple and also rhubarb plate cake were our favourites but also rock buns and coconut castles, iced buns and Bakewell tarts. Mince pies were a must at Christmas.

'There wasn't much I didn't like, but we didn't really get a choice. You either ate what you were given or went hungry. I didn't like liver and onions but that was not on the menu very often. If it was not going to get eaten, then my mother could not afford for it to be wasted. One of my sisters did not like turkey so at Christmas we all told her it was a big chicken, and of course she ate it.

'There was never any drink in the house except at Christmas and then just a few beers, and maybe a bottle of whisky and the obligatory bottle of Harvey's Bristol Cream. That was to offer to anyone that called round. Any drink that was left would still be there the next Christmas.

'My mother used to shop at the Co-op for tins and foodstuff for the store cupboard but went to the high street butcher's and baker's for fresh meat and bread. She then sent me when I was old enough. She also shopped at Fine Fare and Bi-Rite – both no longer in existence.

'As a young child we had many weekend outings, places relatively close by, and, yes, Silloth was one of them along with a run further up the road to Allonby. At Silloth we would walk along the sea front and run up and down the steps to the mainly stony seashore, providing the tide was out, of course. Me and my brother and sisters would collect seashells and sometimes the odd crab or two. We would also dig for anything that might be lurking just below the surface and collect all sorts of snails and other pond life. If we could find a bit of sand we would have competitions to see who could build the best sandcastles, then take great delight in knocking them down. Of course, we all then had to have a paddle in the usually freezing sea, then we would end up running back up to the steps, shivering, to get dried off. Sometimes we would go into the amusement arcade and play on the penny slot machine and bandits with any loose change Mam had put by. If we were lucky we would be treated to a candyfloss.

'We usually took a picnic tea. There would be a bottle of fizzy pop for us kids and the traditional Thermos of tea for the parents. To eat the picnic, quite often we would drive a few miles down the coast along to the sand dunes at Allonby. We'd have an old-fashioned tartan blanket along with a couple of deckchairs. The chairs being for Mam and Dad, we had to sit on the blanket. It would all be spread out on the grass and the picnic would begin. There was usually some sort of scrap between us kids as to who had had the most cakes or biscuits, or who would have the last sandwich. This was quickly sorted out by Dad who would say, "If you lot don't shut up and behave yourselves none of you will get any more." None of us dared argue with Dad, so that was quickly the end of the squabble.

'Another place we used to go for outings was Hammond's Pond, a park which was just a couple of miles away and still within the city. There were rowing boats and we would have come prepared with some stale bread to feed the ducks, running away if they got too close to us. There was a good play park with the usual swings and roundabouts and a huge helter skelter – well, it was huge to us. If my memory serves me correctly, there was an aviary with lots of different birds to look at.

'There were still fields immediately behind our back garden and we would play there and look for brambles so that Mam could bake a cake. Beyond was a railway line that ran across the back of the field. We would sit many a long while collecting train names and numbers from engines like the *Flying Scotsman*.

'All of these places we used to go as children were basically free – apart from making up the picnic – but they provided good fun and lots of exercise and the fresh air that we were always being told we all needed.

Really, I think Mam and Dad just wanted to tire us all out. More often than not most of us fell asleep in the car on the way home.

'We also used to all go to my grandmother's for tea on a Sunday. This was always a feast as she was a great cook and baker of every kind of cake imaginable. Apart from all the goodies, she used to give us each a sixpence. That was a small fortune. You could go the sweet shop twice and still have a halfpenny left. We used to be able to get four fruit salad or black jack chewy sweets for one penny.

'As a child growing up in the fifties and sixties, I think we had a happy fun time. None of it cost our parents very much, which is just as well as generally there was not a lot of spare money. We made our own fun and enjoyed it mostly for free.

'Nowadays, children aren't able to just play outside. Everything outside the house is sort of prearranged and seems to cost so much. We would play tennis or badminton in the street with a makeshift net made from an old bit of washing line, holding it up or tying it to a couple of lamp posts. It was fun and free and encouraged us to use our initiative. Today, the kids have to go to a sports club and everything is there for them.'

Barbara's father did have a car, which was still unusual in the late 1950s and 1960s. During the war, and just afterwards, when Ivy, Dulcie, Dorothy and Jean were growing up, no one in working-class families had a car. The streets were always empty, the better for young boys to play marbles along the gutters or football down the length of the street or for girls to play hopscotch or skipping. No need for parking signs or parking meters, or speed limits and restrictions. No one had a vehicle to park or to speed in. In an ordinary working-class street, whether council houses or terrace rows, if you saw a car parked in the street the chances were it was the doctor come to visit someone poorly. A doctor visiting you at home, that is also now a period piece, as much as totally empty, vehicle-free streets.

By the late fifties, things were picking up a bit economically, with full employment. Barbara's father was a lorry driver, so he was reasonably well paid if he did overtime, and having his own little car was useful to get himself to the lorry depot.

'I can't remember exactly when Dad got his first car. I was quite young at the time, probably around six or seven years of age, so it must have been around 1960. I believe it was an Austin A40, quite a small car, and fairly old, bought second hand. It was black, but then quite a lot of cars of the time were black. He did at one time have a car with a starting handle, but I really can't remember what model it was. That one may have been the Austin, possibly an Austin Cambridge. My memory may be lying to me on his early ones.

'But I do remember him having a car called, I believe, a Vauxhall Ventora. It was a lot bigger than the little Austin. It was white and had classy red leather seats. I think the front seat was called a bench seat, which was one seat rather than two individual seats. I also think it had a column gear change rather than the more traditional gearstick. In those days cars were not fitted with seat belts.

'By the early seventies, probably due to my mother's money management skills, my parents were able to buy a brand-new car. They bought a Ford Zephyr from the local dealership. It was a larger car, which was needed to accommodate all us kids. By this time I would be about eighteen. I seem to remember the car costing the princely sum of £672.

'There were by now a few other neighbours that had cars. It was almost always the husband's car, as they would need it to get to and from work. Not so many women had a car in those days – or could drive. The mums and the kids would either walk into town, and you would see loads of them on a Saturday morning, humping all their shopping back, or they would get the bus into town, depending on the finances at the end each week.'

The big change in Barbara's life came at the age of eleven when it was time to leave her primary school, Pennine Way in Harraby, one of Carlisle's biggest housing estates.

'I knew the Eleven Plus was coming up and looked forward to it. I was confident I would pass, everyone said I would. Let's put it this way, I would have been very disappointed if I hadn't passed. In fact I found it easy.'

There were only two girls in her class who passed for the high school that year, a fairly typical result for a primary school in the heart of a council estate, compared with a primary school like Stanwix, in the north of the city, which was surrounded by private semis and detached houses and where at least half the class each year went on to the high school or the grammar school.

'It was strange to meet girls whose fathers were doctors or dentists, but it didn't bother me, I didn't feel intimidated. If people don't accept me for what I am, then I am not going to bother with them. I had an old head on young shoulders.'

Getting the uniform was a bit of a headache and proved expensive. It was only available at certain shops, like Harker & Bell, which was expensive, but good quality, where the middle-class girls got their uniform, or the Co-op which was a bit cheaper. You were limited to these two or three shops and they kept the prices high.

'But there were no really cheap places, as there are today, like Asda or Tesco. I noticed last week you can buy three polo shirts suitable for school for £3.50, or even less.

'Back in the late fifties and sixties, school clothes were so expensive. I don't know how my mother managed, what with buying the blazer and the badge, which had to be sewn on, plus all the tunics and skirts and gym clothes and thick grey tights, not forgetting the dreaded maroon felt beret. With your grey dress you had to wear grey knickers and maroon knickers with your maroon gym tunic. We had to embroider our names on the back of our gym knickers during the first sewing lesson we had.

'Your dress had to be no more than half an inch off the ground when you knelt down, that was the rule. Modesty, I suppose. You couldn't eat in the streets, not if you were in school uniform, not even a penny ice lolly. We did buy them of course, hiding in a lane on the way to school to suck them.

'If you were caught, the punishment was a loss of house points. The house system was very strong and there was great competition. They were named in Greek – Alpha, Beta, Gamma, Delta.

'Maths, I could still do easily. If I forgot or could not be bothered to do my homework, I could do it in ten minutes on the way to school. But I hated Latin. I couldn't see the point of it. I knew I was never going to use it, all that stuff about *puella habit tunicam* – the girl has a tunic. I think that's right, but maybe not. Amazing I have remembered any of it, after all these years.

'I didn't want to learn it and it has been no use to me in life – though recently I have been looking at the various medicine tablets I have been taking and knowing a bit of Latin has helped me, like *di* means two or double. But at the time, I thought what rubbish, I'm never going to be a doctor, so there's no reason to learn Latin.'

While not liking Latin and some of the other subjects, Barbara did not cause trouble or speak out. She went behind the bike sheds to have a smoke, but so did other girls. 'I did not fear authority, but I liked to comply whenever I could. I never shouted my mouth off, or challenged authority, unless I was very sure of my facts.

'Many of the teachers were old maids and a bit scary, like Miss Haig who had her hair in a plait, a big wart on her face and a moustache. We would poke fun at how she looked behind her back, which was bad. As an adult, I would never do that. Then there was Mrs Murray-Seaforth who was Scottish and very eccentric. You had no idea what she would do or how she would react. She would go down a line and shout VG, VG, VG, VG at every girl, while another time she would go down the line and every one would lose house points.'

After three years, and in what was then called the fourth year, about to make her decisions on what O levels to take, Barbara decided to leave high school. This was most unusual. Girls in the sixties did not do such things, unless they had been expelled or fallen pregnant. Getting to the high school was seen as a passport to higher education, a better life, all the supposed good things. So why give it up?

'I got it into my head that what I wanted to be was a secretary and the high school did not do typing and shorthand. It was all very academic.'

The other element was the political changes taking place. All over the country, comprehensive schools were about to come in. In 1967 in Haringey, an Outer London Borough, they closed thirty-seven grammar schools and secondary moderns overnight and turned them into eleven comprehensives.

In Carlisle in 1968, the long-established, 800-year-old Carlisle Grammar School was joined with two secondary technical schools, the Creighton and Margaret Sewell, to become Trinity, a huge comprehensive.

In 1967, when Barbara made her decision to leave, Carlisle's High School for Girls was still a selective grammar school, though in a year or so, it was to turn into St Aidan's Comprehensive. The changes had not been finalised, but some schools that had earlier been seen as less favoured had already started to gear up. One of them was Morton School, a secondary modern very near where Barbara lived. It was about to turn itself into a comprehensive, at least in name. It had opened a new wing, which offered secretarial and office training. This is partly what attracted Barbara, and made her want to leave the high school.

So in September 1967, along with one other high school girl, she enrolled at Morton School.

'My mother was not 100 per cent pleased. But she said OK then, I could go on condition I stayed on till I was sixteen at the new school and take O levels, which I did. I think I got eleven in all – five Os and seven CSEs at A/B grade. A grade was supposed to count as the equivalent of an O level.'

At the new school, Barbara was seen as a bit of snob, who thought she was 'it' having come from a superior, selective school.

'The girls were not so bad as I knew many of them locally, but some of the teachers were sarcastic. They would actually say in class, "You think you are better than the others because you have come from that place." It took me a while to realise it was true – we were a year ahead in many of the lessons. We stood out, and therefore got picked on. If we were in a group caught smoking, along with loads of others, we would be the ones hauled out, just because we had gone to "that high school".'

Looking back, Barbara thinks today she is on the whole in favour of selection, of competition, and does not think the old Eleven Plus exam was so bad after all. She does not think it made pupils feel like failures if they did not pass, in fact she believes it probably alienated the few people from her sort of council estate who did pass for the high school or grammar school as it separated them from their peer group.

'People have to be treated equally, and made to feel they are of equal importance, even if they are all going to achieve different things in life.

'On the other hand, in life, you have to take your knocks, so starting early in life having some knocks is not all that bad.'

Barbara's first job in life was at thirteen, when she became a newspaper delivery girl, morning and evening.

'After a few months I was "promoted", you could say, deployed in the shop marking up the addresses on the newspapers. This was far preferable to going out in all weathers delivering. At the age of fifteen, was also employed as a Saturday girl in Woolworths. The wage was £1 3d for the day. I cannot remember exactly how much I was paid from the newsagent but think it started at about seven shillings – this would be in 1966/1967. This extra pocket money earned by myself saved my parents from having to give me set pocket money each week. I am sure it also taught me at an early age the value of working for things that I wanted.'

Aged sixteen in 1970, Barbara left school for full-time work, starting in the offices at Pirelli, the tyre factory, though at the time the Carlisle factory was mainly producing slippers. Her first wage was £25 a month.

'I was in the wages department, calculating the gross wage from the hourly rate and the hours worked plus any overtime that may have been due, making up the wages, working out the tax and national insurance to be taken off, and finally handing the wage packets to the employees. I quickly realised that some of the girls on the factory floor, with no O levels, making slippers, were getting twice as much as me, if they were on piecework and doing well.'

So she looked for another office job, this time in an engineering firm, where she felt a bit happier as her pay went up from roughly £6 a week to £8.50p.

Note the 50p. Not ten shillings. In 1971 in the UK, the decimal age arrived and out went shillings and pence. Until then there had been 240 pennies in a pound – denoted by the letter d from the Latin denarius, which of course Barbara would have spotted. There were twenty shillings in a pound – s standing for a shilling, from the Latin solidus. And every shilling contained twelve pennies. Now we had a hundred new pennies, signified by a p, in a pound. Simple.

It had only taken the UK 150 years to make the change. The first movement for decimalisation had started in 1824, influenced by the change in France in 1795 when the decimal franc was introduced, containing a hundred centimes.

Barbara, being good at maths, was well able to cope and understand all the complications, which at first confused so many British people. Barbara has always been interested in money – how to get it, what to do with it, what it can do.

'I always religiously gave a third of my wages each week to my mother. I kept a third to myself and a third I saved. I opened an account at the Cumberland Building Society. In those days, the seventies, the interest rates were about 7–8 per cent.'

As a wage earner, Barbara started buying her own clothes and became interested in fashion and in popular music.

'Mostly I liked to buy clothes at a shop called Van Allen which was next to the old Woolworths store on English Street. They were reasonably cheap and quite fashionable. When I was younger, I could get a dress for about 29s 11d or 39s 11d – which is about £1.50 to £2 in today's money. There was also another shop call Paige's that a lot of young women used.

'Van Allen was next to True Form shoe shop which had reasonably fashionable and reasonably priced shoes. Like dresses, shoes were usually priced around 29s 11d or 39s 11d, or sometimes less in the sales. Then there was the likes of Saxone, which was generally a bit more expensive and sold branded shoes like Hush Puppies. They were probably around 49s 11d or 59s 11d.

'I tended to like classic styles with a hint of current fashion, maybe in the detail or the colour, as they tended to last a bit longer, although of course I occasionally deviated from this.

'I did have platform shoes and of course hot pants, both against my parents' advice. I also longed for a midi skirt and a "crop" top and did get both. The skirt was black and buttoned all the way down the front, but the top I had to knit myself. It was the palest peach colour.

'We all wore nylons with of course a suspender belt. I was not made to wear a corset although I can remember my grandmother lacing up hers and my mother wearing one for a back complaint.

'As a child I was made to wear a liberty bodice, as most young kids still were.

'When miniskirts came in and were all the rage; all us girls wore them and our dads used to say, "You're not going out in that" along with "You can get all that muck off your face". In true teenage fashion, we took the make-up with us and put it on later.

'I did make some of my own clothes from paper patterns, mostly blouses and skirts. We were taught how to do this at school. I was also shown how to sew by my grandmother and often used her old Singer sewing machine, which had a treadle to control the speed.

'I was always doing my hair, it had to be just so. I occasionally used to go to the local hairdresser's, which was located at the back of the newsagent's where I had been a paper girl. They did a good job. When I was feeling flush or wanted something a bit different I might go to one of the more expensive salons in town, but mostly I did my own. My mother and grandmother often used to get me to do home perms for them, using something called Twink or Pin Up. I can't really remember how much it cost at the hairdresser. I think maybe about 10s–15s for a shampoo and set.

'I have tried most styles over the years but my hair has mostly been short. As a child we girls – me and my two sisters – were not allowed to have our hair long. It always had to be a short back 'n' sides, so to speak, for all of us.

'But as a teenager I used to backcomb my hair till it was as high as I could get it, then use loads of hairspray to keep it in place. I also used to perm it myself. I once bought a wash-in-wash-out colour shampoo which was chestnut brown and my brown hair went orange. I washed my hair about ten times that day before it looked sort of OK. I never bought that colour again.

'I enjoyed most of the popular music of the day, the Beatles, the Stones, Marc Bolan, the Who, the Drifters, Union Gap and yes even Cliff Richard, and of course the instrumental music of the Shadows like "Apache". I never went to any pop concerts but did have pictures of Paul McCartney and Marc Bolan.

'As a teenager I used to listen to Radio Caroline and I think Radio Luxembourg. I used to listen mostly on a small pocket-size radio with headphones, usually under the bedclothes when I was supposed to be asleep.

'My favourite film stars were Robert Redford and Paul Newman and also Roger Moore and Sean Connery. I thought they were all good-looking. At the time anyway, when I was young and impressionable...'

Barbara went to dances, coffee bars, mainly with her girlfriends, and through mutual friends started going out with a young forklift driver, David Waugh, who was working at 14 MU. She was eighteen, and he was her first serious boyfriend. 'I was wearing my favourite outfit, my midi skirt and peach top, on a night out at the Border Terrier pub when I was first asked out by David.'

They got engaged in 1973 and married in 1974.

Waugh is a common Cumbrian surname and pronounced 'woff', with no connection with the posher, literary family of Waughs from the south who pronounce their name 'war'.

They rented a small house while they waited for their name to come up on the council list. 'We had no family money on either side, no one to help us financially, so our ambition was to get a council house, but the only ones that came up were in Raffles. I didn't want to move there. It had begun to get a bad reputation by that time. That year forty-two council houses became vacant at Raffles and only four at Morton Park – which was a sign of the changes that were happening.'

They then heard about a new development being planned, some two-bedroom flats £5,950 for a ground floor flat and £6,200 for upstairs.

'They had not yet been built, so all you had to do to secure one was put down £25 on the plot.'

They had £25, which Barbara had got for her twenty-first birthday. The arrangement was that later they had to pay a £300 deposit, 5 per cent of the price.

'I had put our savings from our joint wages in the Cumberland Building Society and I had a small endowment policy which I cashed. We were also entitled to a tax refund, this was "the married man's allowance". Putting everything together we managed to raise the deposit. We then managed to secure a mortgage from the Cumberland, where I had been saving, which came to £28 a month.'

So at the age of only twenty-one, Barbara had become a property owner, unusual for such a young couple at the time with no capital and no family money, one of them in unskilled work, but it was not unknown. There was a housing boom on at the time and mortgages with low deposits were being offered to reliable-sounding couples. Their first child Neill was born in 1976, two years after they were married.

In 1977, when Neill was just seven months old, Barbara went 'up street' one day, into the centre of town in order to go to Granada TV Rentals and pay the weekly rent on their new colour TV. She was paying it in cash, as direct debit had not generally come in and many working people still did not use chequebooks.

Most people by then owned a black and white TV, but colour was new and they were expensive, so people rented. TV rental was a good business to be in. The renters very quickly paid as much as they would have paid for a new TV, but TVs were not as reliable as they soon became, or as cheap, so people feared the cost of repairs and preferred to play safe and rent.

Barbara left her baby at her mother-in-law's, saying she would be back in an hour. She paid the TV rental quickly and then decided to have a quick look round the shops as she still had half an hour to spare.

She chanced to look in the window of the Job Centre, where there was a card offering part-time evening work. The rates sounded quite good, but the name of the firm was not mentioned. She went inside, asked for details, and found out that it was packing biscuits at Carr's. She filled in a form, was asked various questions, a phone call was made, and she was told she could go there and then and have an interview.

She rushed back to her mother-in-law's, said something had come up, but did not give details, asking her mother-in-law if she could look after the baby for another hour or so. Then off she went to the Carr's factory in Caldewgate.

'I was interviewed by Tommy Walker in personnel. He was very pleasant and asked me if I had relations working at Carr's. I hadn't, but lots of my husband's family had worked there. I gave their names, and he seemed to know some of them. My fingers got examined – if you had bitten fingernails you did not get the job.

'I gave my date of birth and other details. When I revealed I had a baby, he asked who would look after the child. I said that as the job was going to be part-time evening work, my husband would look after the baby, when he came home from work. That satisfied him. He said go and get your overalls, you can start next week.'

Barbara rushed back to her mother-in-law's and waited for her husband to arrive home from work. He was due to have his tea at his mother's, as he did once a week. They all had tea together, without Barbara mentioning what had happened.

It was only on the walk home to their little flat, with Barbara pushing the pushchair with the baby that she revealed what she had done.

'By the way, David, I've got myself a job, starting next week.'

'Oh aye,' said David, 'where at, like?'

She told him the details, saying it was just a thirteen-week contract, but that it would enable them to save enough money to buy the £150 G Plan sideboard they had been ogling in the shops. He liked the idea of that, and didn't seem phased by having to look after the baby every evening.

Why had she not told him straight away?

'Oh you don't do that sort of thing with men, well certainly not with David. I knew what he was like. When he came straight from work he didn't like being bombarded with things. A lot of men seem to be like this, they can't take it in. "Let me at least get me coat off, woman, before you start." So I waited my time.

'Usually you plant a few seeds in advance, so when they get round to it, they think it's their idea. It's terrible what we women can do. But this time it had just been a sudden whim. I really had no intention of looking for a job that day. I was just putting in time.

'But I suppose subconsciously I must have been thinking of it. We needed more money, for all the things we wanted – and we had to get it by ourselves. There wasn't the "Bank of Mum and Dad", which so many young couples have today, even ordinary working people. You had to make your own arrangements about things like babysitting, which is why Dave had to do it. There were few nurseries and you certainly didn't get help paying for them. Unlike today. They are dumping babies all the time today, what with their breakfast class or after school clubs. I always gave my own children their breakfast and picked them up from school, even though I was working.

'There was also no maternity leave. It was just being introduced – so when I had finished work to have my baby in 1976 I wasn't paid. There was a grant of £25 and an allowance for eighteen weeks – eleven weeks before the birth and seven weeks after, then there was nothing. My job was not guaranteed for when I came back. Family Allowance had not come in either yet – you only got that for a second child, and it was done as a tax allowance against your husband's earnings.'

Family Allowance had been introduced in 1946, worth five shillings a week per child, but not for the oldest child – just for the others. It was in 1977 that Child Benefit was introduced for all children, including the eldest. In 1979 mothers received £4 for every child. The big change, the one that really mattered, was that Child Benefit was paid directly to the mother, which was a huge benefit, giving all mothers more independence, even for those who might well have gone on to spend it on clothes or treats for themselves.

'I think working women have it easier today, whether it's those who want to do ordinary work or those who want to have a "proper" career. The government actively encourages them and gives them help. Mothers in my day, back in the early seventies, with young children, had to do it all on their own, get our husbands or mothers to help out, not rely on the state to make it easy.'

So on 20 June 1977, Barbara started work on the factory floor at Carr's, assuming it would be just for thirteen weeks. She was not bothered about any ideas of it being beneath her, despite having previously been in office work. She was thinking only of the money, which she considered excellent for Carlisle.

She was to get a basic £18.07 a week working part-time for just over twenty-one hours a week, plus £4.52 per week for what was called a flat rate payment, according to the contract she signed. The one-page contract of employment was from 'United Biscuits Limited (Carr's of Carlisle)' and described her job title as 'process worker'. It stated that she had to join the General and Municipal Workers Union. Another clause warned that 'in cases of serious misconduct, the right of immediate dismissal is reserved'.

The big attraction for Barbara was the thought of earning around £22 a week part-time, which was almost as much as her husband was earning working full-time as a driver. He was on only £34, yet putting in twice the number of hours. Just the previous year, working full-time in the office at the engineering firm, Barbara had been getting only £27. So £22 for part-time at Carr's seemed excellent, though at this stage she did not know exactly what she would be doing.

Sufficient, though, so she hoped, to secure that highly desirable G Plan sideboard...

Chapter 13

Ann

Ann in her twenties, still working as a hairdresser

Ann, another post-war baby, four years older than Barbara, was born into a family of Carr's workers. Her mother and father both worked there, as had her uncle and her great-grandfather. She has a photograph of him from the 1880s in a flat cap and with a big bushy moustache, standing in the factory with a couple of cats. He acted as an official rat catcher, while working in the boiler room. Ann suspects the cats did most of the rat catching.

Not surprisingly, as a young girl growing up, she had no intention of working at Carr's. While at school, her ambition was to become a hairdresser.

Ann was born on 1 September 1949, and brought up on the Raffles estate, the traditional home over the decades since the war of thousands of Carr's employees.

She went to Newtown Primary School and remembers the Eleven Plus with horror. She was never good with tests or examinations, but her main fear was the thought of being split from her friends. 'That's what the Eleven Plus did – separate you from friends you had been with since the age of five.'

Fortunately, she did not pass and progressed to Ashley Street Girls, the school Ivy had attended some twenty years earlier. And just as Ivy did, she remembers the sweet smell of the Carr's factory.

'We had this really strict teacher, Mrs Templeton, and I was terrified of her. She once told me to take off a signet ring, which I had been given as a Christmas present by my mother. Now I knew jewellery was not allowed at school, or earrings, but for some reason signet rings were. I knew the rules and would not have disobeyed them. I would have been frightened to do anything not allowed. But she ordered me to take it off. It wouldn't come off, so I went to the lavatories and tried to get it off with soap. Still it wouldn't come off. I was in agony and started crying. In the end it did, but I can still feel the pain and terror of trying to get that bloody signet ring off.'

Ann considers she had a fairly idyllic childhood in the Raffles, living in Raffles Avenue in the 1950s with her parents and her younger brother Keith. It was still at that time, as far as she was concerned, a safe, pleasant, happy place. 'When I was growing up, people didn't lock their doors. You could go off to Silloth for the day and leave your door unlocked. And if it rained, your neighbour would come and take your washing in. Of course there were some poor people. My gran used to say, "We hadn't much, but they had nowt." But everybody tried to help each other. My old clothes were given to families who couldn't afford new ones, and no one took offence at being helped.

'My mother did most of the family cooking when I was growing up. She would shop at the local butcher's for meat, sausages, eggs, etc. and use the local Co-op for general things. She would make stews, tattiepot, mince and dumplings. In winter there would be homemade soup and always a Sunday roast. Summertime was salads, new potatoes. Dad didn't do much cooking at home because he worked shifts. When I was young I didn't like stews and wasn't keen on veg. We did have alcohol at Christmas and if we had family parties.'

With both parents working, their family was relatively well off, having enough to pay for Ann to go on a school trip to Austria. 'Mind you, it only cost £10. We went all the way by bus, boat, and bus, and stayed in a real hotel. It was wonderful.'

As a girl she joined the Brownies, moving on to the Guides and went to meetings connected with St

Luke's church. She made campfires and did Bob a Job. She was also a member of the library, the children's library at first, getting books from a mobile library which came round the estate, mostly books by Enid Blyton. When she got older she was in Morton Library and also went into Carlisle to Tullie House – Carlisle's major Jacobean building which had been converted into a museum and public library.

At home, her father got the *Daily Mirror* delivered every day plus the *Sunday Post*. Her mother got *Woman's Own* and the *People's Friend*, all of which Ann read when growing up.

'I loved "The Broons" in the *Sunday Post* and used to get the *Broons Album* every year for Christmas. I remember reading the letters in the *Sunday Post*. There seemed to be such a lot of them.'

Ann applied to be a hairdresser the moment she left school in 1964 and waited for an opening. In the early 1960s there was plenty of work around, but hairdressing had suddenly becoming highly popular for working-class girls. Mary Quant and Vidal Sassoon had made the latest fashions available to all and girls everywhere wanted to look good and up to date, even at the risk of being known as dolly birds.

After six months of looking, she was taken on as an apprentice hairdresser at Dorothy's in Spencer Street, in the middle of the town, round the corner from the main post office and the main cinema, the Lonsdale. Her wages were £1 17s 6d a week. Her apprenticeship was for three years, plus two years during which she was termed an Improver.

The salon had around fifteen staff, was busy and bustling, with a wide range of clientele, including local shop owners and lots of hard-working girls from nearby factories, including a lot of Carr's workers. 'You could smell them when you did their hair – their clothes smelled of biscuits, a sweet sickly smell, so you knew they'd just come from work.'

Dorothy, the owner of the salon, was considered a hard taskmaster, and the girls used to warn each other when they could hear her heels clipping towards them, but she was liked and admired.

Ann was known as Anita at work, because there was another girl already there called Ann, and it was as Anita she did some modelling. She was told one day she had good hair and was chosen by Joseph, Dorothy's son, along with several other girls, to be models when the salon entered hairdressing competitions.

'That was so exciting, going down to London. We didn't get paid, as such, just our normal wages, plus expenses. We did win a prize in a world championship one year, I think around 1965. I wasn't actually the model that day.

'I had my hair done every colour you can think of

at one time – red, green, blue, everything, and in every sort of style. My mother would say to me, "You are not going out like that!" And I didn't really, not in Carlisle. It was too much for Carlisle. If I was going out in town and was having my hair done at work, I would tell them I was going out in town, so not to make it too fashionable.'

Ann loved most of the sixties pop groups, but the Beatles most of all. 'I found the Stones a bit loud, a bit bashing, but in fact the Stones were the group I did manage to see when they came to Carlisle. And they were brilliant.' The Rolling Stones came to Carlisle once in the sixties, at the ABC Lonsdale on 17 September 1964 when they did two performances.

The Beatles appeared twice in Carlisle the year earlier while on their early English tours. On 8 February 1963, they played at the Lonsdale with Helen Shapiro, aged sixteen, top of the bill. Ann was just thirteen at the time. She queued up for ages with some schoolfriends, but they failed to get any tickets. The Beatles returned eight months later on 21 November 1963 – which was the concert that the young Carr's worker had managed to get into and wrote about in the *Topper Off*. Once again Ann failed to get tickets, despite queuing for several hours.

That first time the Beatles came to Carlisle has passed into Beatles lore. They were staying in the Crown and

Mitre, Carlisle's smartest hotel, and after their performance at the Lonsdale, they had gone back to their hotel and wandered into the ballroom. Ringo started jiving with Helen Shapiro while the other Beatles spotted the buffet and started helping themselves.

They had not realised they had chanced upon one of the social events of the Carlisle calendar, the annual dinner dance of Carlisle Golf Club. Everyone was in evening dress. The Beatles were all scruffy. A golf club official eventually spotted these ill-dressed young interlopers and speedily ejected them.

The story made the front page of most of the national papers next day, though the wording of headlines referred to 'Helen Shapiro and her instrumental backing group the Beatles'.

When they returned to Carlisle in November, they were top of the bill this time with number one hits behind them – but they still stayed once again at the Crown and Mitre, holding no grudges.

Nor did Ann, despite not getting tickets. She joined the Beatles Fan Club and subscribed to *Beatles Monthly*, which appeared from August 1963 to 1969. Paul McCartney was her favourite and she had his photograph stuck on the inside of her wardrobe door. Her other pin-up in the sixties was Sean Connery in his James Bond films. She also liked Elvis and saw all his films.

'I loved Sundays after Radio One began [in 1967] and you had the top thirty or the top forty, or whatever it was. We were all desperate each week to find out who was on top.'

Once she had started work in 1964, Ann had money to buy her own clothes. 'Carlisle had lots of boutiques in the sixties, well, I thought we had. I spent a lot of time looking round them. Eve Brown, that was one I went to a lot. And I went to Stead and Simpson for shoes. I did buy stilettos, when they came in, though my mother was against them. They were so uncomfortable, having to push your toes into the pointy bits.

'I also bought platform heels when they became fashionable. I was a bridesmaid once and I insisted I was going to wear my platforms, even though they were hell to wear and you either fell over or they came off. All the bridesmaids had to wear long dresses, so I was able to use elastic bands under my dress to keep the platforms in place, tying them round the ankles.

'Going out to dances, you would wear panty girdles and suspender belts to hold up your nylon stockings. I bought my nylons from Marks & Spencer – American Tan they were called. I can't quite remember when tights came in, but they were a huge change.'

The general use of tights by young women was a great relief for most of them, though men rather missed suspender belts, if they ever got to see them, which was rare back in the sixties, at least in Carlisle. But miniskirts did focus on legs, which was some sort of compensation.

'I loved miniskirts – and I also liked maxi dresses when they came in. I suppose my favourite style when I was young was wearing a mini skirt with knee-high boots, wet-look boots they were called, covered in a sort of plastic.

'I studied all the pop stars to see what fashions they were wearing, like Cilla Black and Sandie Shaw. Later on I probably loved Lady Diana best. She always seemed very fashionable.

During the sixties, Ann went to lots of dances and had good times on package holidays with her girl-friends. Aged nineteen, in a holiday snap taken in Majorca with some of her girlfriends, she can clearly be seen to be sporting a beehive, still dead smart in Carlisle.

The carefree, good times with the girls came to a sudden end in 1973 when at the age of twenty-four she fell pregnant. She knew the relationship wasn't going anywhere, but she wanted to keep the baby.

'I was so scared and didn't know how to tell my mam and dad. I couldn't tell me mam, as I knew what she would say. I told the mother of a friend first, and she said I had to tell my mother.

'At work, we were having some new uniforms made for all the staff. Until then we all wore sort of blue smocks but we were now going to wear smarter, more fashionable and tighter pink uniforms. I knew my bump would soon be showing if I wore the new uniform, so I said don't bother with me, I'll stick to the old outfit for the moment. All the other girls immediately went into the new smart outfit.

'Dorothy had been to Eastbourne on her annual holiday and then popped into Blackpool on the way back, where she always had her fortune told. The fortune-teller said that when she got back, one of her staff would look different – and have something to tell her. She didn't know of course what that meant.'

When Dorothy got back, she immediately noticed that Ann was the only one in the old uniform. She took Ann by the arm and led her up into what she sometimes called her office, though it was really just the wig room.

'Are you OK, Ann?' she asked.

'I'm fine thanks, Dorothy.'

'Are you sure, pet?'

'Yes thanks.'

'Is there not something you need to tell me, pet?'

Ann shook her head, but was clearly on the verge of tears. Dorothy then explained what the fortune-teller had told her, which now made sense, as she had guessed Ann's condition.

So it all came out – and Dorothy put her arms round Ann and was kind and comforting, but said she had to tell her mother.

'My mother was really upset. She tried to persuade me to have a termination. In those days, there was a shame and disgrace about unmarried mothers.

'My dad, he was always the quiet one. He did support me. But he did say to my aunty that he was surprised – because of my age. "At twenty-four, you would think she would have had more sense, but aye well, we are where we are so we'll have get on wid it, like..."'

The baby, a boy, was born in 1974 at the Fusehill maternity hospital in Carlisle, where most Carlisle women gave birth at that time.

'He was born at 5.15 and 5.15 – I will always remember the coincidence. Born at 5.15 in the morning weighing exactly five pounds fifteen ounces.'

She had been going to call him Matthew, but changed her mind the moment the baby was shown to her – and named him Adrian, a name that had just come into her head, for no apparent reason.

'My mother adored him from the moment I got him home. He was her golden boy.'

Ann was still living at home, but worked Saturdays at the salon when her mother could help out looking after the baby. Dorothy then fell ill and the business was sold, so Ann moved to another salon, not far away.

When Adrian was five, Ann got a council house; the stigma of being an unmarried mother had lessened and officialdom was recognising that single mothers had needs and rights.

In 1991 Ann was working full-time at the new salon, picking up Adrian from school at three o'clock. With Christmas coming up and needing a bit more money, she looked around for another part-time job.

'Carr's was the obvious place. I had the family connection and the money was good, about the best in Carlisle for unskilled work.'

She had her nails checked, as per usual, and passed, but some others girls, applying at the same time, were turned away, told to come back when their nails had grown.

'No one ever explained to you why they had this passion for short nails – but I later heard the theory was that if you bit your nails down to the quick, then bacteria could get in. I don't know whether that's true or not.'

Her family tradition of service to Carr's naturally played a big part in being taken on. Not many, after all, can boast they are descended from a nineteenth-century Carr's biscuit works rat catcher…

'But the reason I applied was because they were taking extra staff on for the Christmas rush. So I only got taken on as a temporary, for three months. That was all I intended to do, to get a bit of extra money.'

And the reason they were taking on extra staff at Christmas time goes back over a hundred years, even before her great-grandfather worked there.

Christmas had always been a great time for biscuits. Early Victorian workers had been starved of much that was sweet and sickly, except on special or festive occasions. Their normal diet was boiled beef and carrots, plus potatoes, possibly turnips. There were no afters, no little sweet biscuits to go with their afternoon break in the fields. Only the well-off had fancy biscuits to dip in their post-dinner wine glasses.

Once the industrialisation of biscuit manufacturing began, the price fell. Biscuits, after all, are cheap to make, compared with most cakes. Biscuits are basically flour, fat and sugar. Creams for filling and cocoa or ginger to add an extra taste came in later, when the competition hotted up, but inside every fancy biscuit there was still a basic one, quietly and modestly lying there underneath the icing, made of the stuff they have always been made of.

Biscuits don't require eggs, which can be expensive and awkward to transport, or fruits, fresh or dried, which can be expensive and seasonal. Once you have a successful biscuit, you can control and standardise production and keep turning it out for ever, till tastes change or someone offers a better, tastier bite.

Once biscuits were mass-produced, they were priced and packaged and marketed to suit all pockets. The tuppenny packets, which Ivy was put on when she first started, had been a mainstay of all biscuit manufacturers since the late nineteenth century.

Long before therapists thought of clever things to say to us in time of need or despair, the solution in most British households and in most families to a moment of stress or tension or disappointment was to say, 'There there, I'll make you a nice cup of tea and get you a biscuit, you'll feel much better.'

Looking at a plate of biscuits, deciding which to scoff first, or being offered your choice from a whole tin, being allowed to pick any you like, was solace in itself for tired minds and bodies. 'Go on, it won't hurt, I've heard biscuits are good for you', so mothers have said for decades. Almost immediately, it took your mind off your woes. Biscuits as therapy, it does work.

In work situations, biscuits have also eased the pain at moments of stress, but essentially in offices and factories they have served as a treat, a reward for good behaviour, putting up with two hours of some boring repetitious job, or some dreadful boss or superior. Biscuits in offices and other workplaces are a communal, bonding activity, particularly when bought jointly by the workers, although far-sighted and benevolent bosses might put them on the slate, as worker expenses. On a special day, such as someone's birthday, a cake might be involved, but the workaday snack is a biscuit. After all, cakes need a knife to cut them, and perhaps a napkin, a plate, and even a fork with which to eat them. Biscuits can be passed around and eaten right out of the packet.

The tradition of mid-morning coffee and afternoon tea had been a feature of the leisured classes in the eighteenth century, but in the nineteenth and twentieth centuries, the habit had spread to the growing middle classes. The change in habits was helped by the decline in large cooked breakfasts before a working day and also fewer people having hot, three-course lunches. Those who spent the first hour of their working day on a commuter train didn't really need or deserve a full English to set them up. And while at work, there was often no time for a proper lunch. Instead, why not fit in a welcoming morning and afternoon biscuit break?

The biscuit industry, helped by the cocoa and drinking chocolate makers, around the beginning of the twentieth century, managed to suggest to the nation that there was a third period in the day when biscuits might be in order – a late-evening pre-bed drink, such as cocoa or Ovaltine, accompanied by a biscuit. A late repast, so the advertising proclaimed, would help to ward off 'night-time starvation', a concept and worry most people had never realised they might suffer from. Very clever and ingenious.

The phrase 'that takes the biscuit' was also cleverly used and adopted by the biscuit spin-doctors. Origi-nally, it is thought to have referred to cake, not biscuits, and goes back to the plantation days in the USA. The black slaves had an event in which they walked round a table containing a cake and the one voted the most stylish would take the cake. In ancient Greece there was also a tradition where the best fighter was given a reward of a special sweetmeat.

Biscuits are usually the first items any child learns to make, as the ingredients are simple and the baking process quick. Children, who have a sweet tooth anyway, therefore learn to love biscuits from an early age, and the simple act of making and even icing your own biscuits is an activity that becomes associated with childhood.

Biscuits, as a treat or a snack, have survived changing economic and social conditions and how and where people work. But who could have predicted that biscuits would not just be something nice to nibble at home or work, but would turn out to be perfect gifts? J.D. Carr would have been so pleased to see the rise of biscuits as presents.

The development of special tins did of course aid their appeal as gifts, making them extra desirable and worthy of being given and received, but it was still the contents that mattered most. If you could organise enough variety and richness and wonder inside a tempting tin of assorted biscuits, pack them suggestively and alluringly, with the possibility of even lovelier biscuits lurking under the top rows, then you had an Aladdin's cave of biscuits, a veritable feast, a vast variety.

It was roughly around 1900, and then right up to the Second World War, and then again in recent years, that biscuit assortments became the answer to every Christmas present. Not the main present, but the most suitable gift to give to an aunt or uncle, a grandma or great-aunt, a child or teenager or to a whole family. How could they disappoint, containing as they did something nice for everyone, at every age and stage?

Biscuit manufacturers like Carr's put an enormous amount of energy and resources and invention into creating suitably exotic and alluring gift boxes of biscuits, tempting the public with exciting tins, often with new lines, new sensations alongside the old favourites, all done especially for the Christmas markets. Well-established lines, such as shortbreads, always get a makeover for Christmas, smartened up, making them somehow more special and luxurious and well, Christmassy.

Books have always sold well at Christmas, a quarter of the year's sales going in the last month, with publishers bringing out their best, most commercial, most enticing products for the Christmas market. Same with biscuits and for similar reasons. Biscuits, like books, make simple but universally acceptable presents.

For over the last hundred years, Christmas became

the best time of the year for all biscuit manufacturers. Each year thousands of temporary workers, like Ann, were grateful for the Christmas rush. It gave them some extra work, even if most of them assumed it would only be for a short time. So Ann started what she thought would be a short break on the shortbreads...

Chapter 14
Barbara

Barbara, our other post-war baby, was struck on her first day at Carr's by how many old buildings there were. She had known about the existence of Carr's all her life but had not been aware of its history, or that the factory had been built in 1837. She had not worked on a factory floor before, being an ex-high school girl. She had worked in an office, till she left to have her first baby.

'The old brick walls had been painted white, the floors were concrete, there seemed to be loads of machinery and it felt hot and noisy. But I had only come for the money, so that didn't matter too much.

'But I don't really remember now what I thought of Carr's when I first walked in. I do remember thinking it was not what I expected – whatever that may have been, cos I don't really know.

'It appeared to be a dreary-looking, old unforgiving sort of building and was very noisy once you got on to the shop floor. But once you were "placed" on a job it was far from dreary. The craic – Carr's craic – kept you going through the mainly repetitive and boring task of packing the biscuits, plus it was good to talk to adults for a few hours after being at home with only two small children to look after all day.'

Barbara remembers the date she started: 20 June 1977, aged twenty-four. As ever, she is precise on dates, facts and figures and especially monies. She was given a nylon overall though linen ones came in later – and a cap she describes as lacy. There had been other organisational changes by the time she arrived. The rank of charge hand and supervisor had become the same thing, but they still wore pink, while above them was a forewoman who wore navy blue.

She met Ivy, as most newcomers did, the old hand who had been there for so long, knew it all, and helped with training the new girls. Dulcie, for a while, was

Barbara's ID card issued when she joined Carr's in 1978

Barbara's timekeeper. Her charge hand when she first began was Jean. Alas, none of them ever seemed to have had their photos taken together at work, or even singly, in their overalls and hats. Carr's does not seem to have approved of photographs being taken in the workplace by the workers – except for official photographs for the annual report. Our six women, like most of the population of the time, tended not to have their photos taken regularly anyway, except on their holidays, and then the pitures usually turned out faint and blurry. Most ordinary working people did not have their own cheap cameras till the 1960s.

At first Barbara was put on Shorties. A conveyor belt brought the biscuits from the ovens. They had to be flicked over by a flip roller and stacked. They were then picked up, between about fifteen and twenty at a time, and fed into a wrapping machine. Other girls would take them from the wrapping machine and put them in boxes, eight or ten packets at a time, until the box was filled. The box was then taped and palletised, which just meant putting on pallets for the barrowmen to barrow away.

'You were told you had to keep the wrapping machine loaded all the time, or time and money would be lost. Jean, my charge hand, was tough but positive. "You've got to be faster," she would say, "or you won't make the grade."

'It was boring and monotonous, but physically it was not too tiring, but then, I was a young fit woman at the time.'

After a while, she was moved on to small Table Water Biscuits, where it was hotter as they were nearer the ovens.

'You had to straighten them by hand, which only took a second, but you still got blisters from the heat if you were not careful. If you complained, the charge hand would say, "You shouldn't hold them long enough to get blisters."

'Gloves were available but most girls didn't wear them. You were more dexterous with bare fingers. Now of course you have to wear gloves, all the time. You are not supposed to touch anything with bare hands.'

After her thirteen weeks trial period was up, she and her husband David had bought their G Plan sideboard. She was offered a permanent contract, so decided to stay.

'I had got used with the money. As one of the lasses told me in that first week, if you survive to take your first pay packet home, you're hooked.

'I was on water biscuits with Ann McVitie as my charge hand. No, no connection with the biscuit firm. We were told she was married to George McVitie, the Carlisle United footballer, but she never talked about it.

'The lasses on the team were either like me, young mothers with young children, or older married women with their children almost grown up. The older ones always looked after the younger, as I was looked after when I joined.

'I discovered I had to hold my tongue at certain times, not make personal remarks about people. You might be bad-mouthing someone and then discover it was their aunty or cousin. Carr's was full of families who had worked there for decades. It was one reason you didn't have strikes. They knew if the factory closed, all of their family would be out of work.

'There was great loyalty for each other and the firm, you would do anything to help someone else, but it was really based round the factory. You didn't socialise much after work, but we did have some great Christmas party nights out. Everyone had their own family and children to worry about, but when there was a funeral, even of someone who had not worked there for years, hundreds would turn out. If someone was ill, we'd take turns to go and visit. There was a family culture. You had your ups and downs, but we all pulled together.'

In 1979, Barbara had a second child, Sharon. She says she had timed it to get the maximum tax advantage, as she had done with her first child. 'If you have them towards the end of the year, you got a good tax rebate, so I had one in November and one in December. I know it sounds awful, but I had planned it that way.'

She had gone on the Pill just before she got married, and carried on with it till she was twenty-five. 'When I was trying for Sharon, I always said if I didn't have a second by the time I was aged twenty-five, that would be it, no more.

'Three years after the birth of Sharon, I got sterilised, by which time I was twenty-eight. I could have asked David to have a vasectomy but something told me that was not for him. Anyway, I have always preferred to be in control. At least of myself.'

She got no maternity leave or wages while away from work giving birth to her first child but did get maternity leave and pay with her second child. Even so she returned to work just three months afterwards, having set her sights on moving up the property ladder.

In 1978 they had sold their small flat for £8,500 – having bought it for £5,950, therefore making a profit of almost 50 per cent in just four years. They then bought a Link house for £11,600, taking on a further mortgage. 'Link was just a posh name for a new terrace house, but it was a whole house, with three bedrooms, so we felt we had achieved something. But in my mind, the next stage was to have our own semi. So we were still saving just as hard and still needing the two wages.'

Her husband, since the day they had married, had handed over his entire wage packet to Barbara – as her own father had done. 'I just copied their system. My dad would hand it over and my mum would put it all in a tin with little divisions. She would say that's for rent, that's for gas, that's for food – and here's your pocket money. It seemed to work. I have done the same pretty much all our working lives.'

Barbara has always been the financial brains in their family, having been an ace at maths while at school, unlike David, who had no interest in money or knowledge of mortgages and interest rates, not even having a chequebook. He left it all to Barbara. Fortunately she turned out to be excellent at it. David's interest was in cars and with Barbara's wages coming in, he was soon able to indulge himself a little, eventually buying himself a Jaguar XJ.

Barbara worked for the next four years on the factory floor, packing biscuits, and enjoyed the company of the other lasses.

'The winters were OK but the summers can get very hot. Sticky knicker weather we called it. On really humid days you would come into work with your clothes already sticking to you, so it was terrible if you had to work on anything too near the ovens. You just sweated all day long.

'When I first started working at Carr's I used to get the bus to work and back every night. Sometimes my husband would give me a lift there and I would just get the bus home. In December 1981 I passed my driving test and was then able to use the family car to get to and from work. This was much more convenient. When the shift finished the only thing on everyone's mind was to get to the clocking-out area and punch your time card and head to the locker area and get home as quickly as possible.

'Working with women was quite good, really, as there was a good mix across the generations. The older lasses often looked out for the younger ones. Having said that, a lot of the older more experienced workers often thought they knew everything, that they could do the job better that the young ones, which wasn't always true. The younger girls also looked out for the older lasses, especially the ones nearing retirement and were maybe struggling slightly to keep up. Basically, underneath any surface bickering or bitching that might go on, when it came right down to it we all really did look after each other.'

Most of the other biscuit girls, and most factory workers, are content to stay at the same level, receive their wages and not have to take home any thoughts or stresses connected with work. That's why they are doing it – simply for the money. Barbara was doing it for the money, but she was ambitious for more. Which meant she soon began to think of promotion.

After four years packing, she applied and was

accepted to be a quality controller. QC, so it was called, for which she got to wear a red collar on her overall. It was not looked upon as a greatly desirable job, so not many applied.

'It wasn't much more money, just a pound or two a week, but was more interesting and varied. You went round weighing the biscuits, picking them at random to check if they were lightweight or not. You also checked the date codes and other things. If they were light, you put up a "Hold" notice, a yellow A4 card which said "Hold For Audit". You might be holding up fifty to sixty boxes that had already been packed, if you had found one packet light, so you weren't very popular. Piecework had stopped by the time I started, but it still ruined their targets if you held things up.'

The other thing Barbara had to look out for was any foreign bodies, such as a bit of metal or plastic which had got into the biscuits. By now, metal detectors had come in and all packets and boxes had to go through them automatically. If the machine started pinging, the QC had to stop the work, find the foreign body, and then work out at what stage and when it might have happened, checking when the line was last declared safe.

'It was usually to do with something happening in the oven. There was a wire mesh conveyor band in most ovens. The mixing area was another critical control point. Bits could come off one of the belts. It rarely ever happened, but now with health and safety coming in, you had to check everything and get to the bottom of it.'

The major health and safety changes in the UK started with the Health and Safety at Work Act of 1974. It was long overdue in industrial plants generally as lax methods and supervision had grown up. Lack of proper rules, for example, had led to many North Sea divers being killed or injured. There were dramatic stories in the newspapers and then long-drawn-out investigations. In the mining industry as well, still going strong, corners had been cut and lives endangered. Then there was the problem of working with asbestos, which no one seemed to have realised was a potential killer. The effects of radioactivity in the nuclear industry had also not been fully understood.

By the 1980s, health and safety procedures were being laid down in all industries and all workplaces, leading to a small army of health and safety enforcers, lots of work for lawyers and an avalanche of posters and warnings in the workplaces as the bosses covered themselves, just in case. In a biscuit factory, the worry was not just injury to any of the workers, which of course did happen, but of greater concern was possible injury or damage to customers caused by eating something dodgy in a Carr's product, leading to legal problems and a dramatic fall in sales.

So as a QC, Barbara's job was vital. She was allowed to walk into any of the individual plants – as the various departments were called – and do a random test and call a halt if necessary. Not the sort of job that many ordinary working women want to do, especially if they're only in it for the pocket money, or extra cash for Christmas.

'I always got the same reply every time I opened the big doors and walked into Icing Plant. "You can fuck off right away." That's what the charge hand would say as soon as I entered. It didn't upset me. It was just banter.

'I didn't swear, not till I started at Carr's, but I heard a lot of it. Not from all the women, just a minority who seemed to swear all the time. Nothing personal. They were not swearing at you, just when telling you something. "I went to fucking Tesco and got some fucking cigarettes and then met my fucking husband..." They didn't know they were swearing, half the time.'

Barbara was a QC for five years. Then in 1987 she put in for another promotion, this time to that of charge hand/supervisor.

There was a bit more money, but she was still in touch with the workers on the lines, not stuck in some office.

'One of the ways to say thank you to a team who had worked well was to let them go for an extra smoke or a cup of tea for ten minutes. It would reward them with an extra break, but of course the work still had to go on, the conveyor belt was still rolling. So I would stand in the line in her place, doing her job. So even as a charge hand, you were still doing physical work.'

As a charge hand, one of the things she had to do was sort out any rows or arguments between the girls. There was occasional shouting and swearing, though rarely did it lead to hair-pulling or punching, though that was not unknown.

'You had to act quickly, when you saw it flaring up. "Right, you stand over there, I'll talk to you later." Then you would investigate what had happened.

'For fighting you could be immediately suspended, but usually a row just resulted in a warning. After three warnings, then you could be subject to some form of more serious discipline.'

One of the more serious breaches of conduct was ignoring SOP – Standard Operating Procedure – not doing something that should have been done, even if it did not result in an accident, though often it did.

'Some of the girls didn't care. You would say, "Right, you are now suspended, go home." They would say, "Not bothered, it's a sunny day, better at home than this effing place..."

'They would stay at home for three days on full pay while the case was investigated, for of course until that was done it wasn't known if they were guilty or not.

'Another serious breach of conduct was hitting a charge hand, a manager or another team member, or coming into work drunk. For that you could get sacked immediately. That was considered gross misconduct.

'On the whole, I can't remember many serious incidents that I had to deal with personally. In the main it was just relatively minor squabbles.'

Chapter 15
Ann

Ann, the single mother, had only planned to work at Carr's as a Christmas extra for three months maximum, doing the evening shift, from six to ten, going straight there from her full-time job at the hair salon. Her son Adrian, now sixteen, was happy enough to go to his grandmother's for his tea.

'It was very daunting going to a work in a factory as I had never worked in one before. Even though my mother had worked there for so long, I had never actually been to it. All the different departments were still separate, like the chocolate room, or the Bourbon room, not under one roof as they later became. Going down that long corridor, it was like Spaghetti Junction – with rooms and doors and little corridors and yards suddenly leading this way and that. There seemed to be so many different areas. I got lost numerous times. It was also very noisy.

'I got the bus to work each day. They were always full at finishing times with everybody rushing out of the factory to catch their bus.

'Lots of women working together could cause problems on occasions as sometimes personalities clashed, but most of the time it was OK.'

At Carr's, her charge hand for a while was Barbara, beginning to zoom up the career ladder as well as the property ladder. Unlike our women who were born pre-war, both Ann and Barbara – born 1949 and 1953 – seemed keen from the beginning to better themselves, at work and at home.

Ann's three months extended to two years – over which time she still did two jobs. It meant that during the working week she hardly saw Adrian. She would go straight from the hair salon to the Carr's factory, there being no time in between to go home. She left her house at 8.30 each morning and did not return till 10.30 at night. But it did mean she was earning good money, which of course she needed as a single mum.

After two years at Carr's, Ann managed to save enough for a deposit to make an offer for her council house. The Right to Buy legislation had come in under the Housing Act of 1980 and is considered to have been one of Mrs Thatcher's major achievements. It had first been proposed in the Labour manifesto of 1959 but Labour had lost, so it was forgotten for a while. Under Mrs Thatcher's legislation, you could get a discount depending on how long you had been a tenant in the house to compensate for all the rent you had paid.

In 1980, Mrs Thatcher managed a much publicised photo opportunity when she handed over the keys to the very first council tenant purchaser, the Patterson family from Romford in Essex. They had lived in the house for eighteen years, which qualified them for a 40 per cent discount and they were able to buy their house for £8,315. Since 1980, it is estimated that two million council tenants in the UK have bought their own houses – many of them subsequently being sold on at a good profit. It was in 1993 that Ann acquired her council house, at a price of £18,760 on a twenty-five-year mortgage. She then decided to give up hairdressing and work at Carr's full-time. When Adrian left school he eventually started working at Carr's as well.

For her first two years at Carr's, Ann was on Bourbons. Ann found it quite hot working on Bourbons, as they were near the ovens, though it was nowhere near as hot as on the water biscuits. The difference being that the Bourbons and custard creams, unlike the water biscuits, went through a cooling process straight out of the oven, before being conveyed along to the packers. Having cream put inside them, they needed to be cooled and solidified before being handled and packaged.

Ann worked with three other girls, picking up the Bourbons and feeding them into a wrapping machine. The biscuits came at them in a constant stream on divided tracks, like miniature railway lines. You had to keep on top of your particular track, emptying it as quickly as possible, then feeding the wrapping machine. Sometimes a machine would stop, break down, or one of the little tracks get blocked, so they had to hope one of the other girls would help you out to clear the blockage and avoid any biscuits being wasted. When that happened, the biscuits began running off the end of the line for all to see.

'It paid to be good friends with all of the girls. You relied on them to help because if you had a problem everything would pile up.

'I never knew why they didn't have automatic packing machines – some machinery to pick up the biscuits and put them in the wrapping machine. I am sure they had been invented by now, after all these decades. But they would have been expensive, so I suppose that was the reason. Girls were cheaper.'

One day, her uncle, who was a shop steward, asked Ann if she would like to be a shop steward too. She said no, definitely not.

'During all those years in hairdressing, I had nothing to do with unions. They didn't exist, in salons, and we all seemed to survive OK.

'But my uncle came back a few months later, saying they were desperate to have a woman shop steward. Could I not just give it a try?'

So she agreed and became one of ten shop stewards at the Carr's factory, representing the GMB.

The union is a result of various mergers over the years, starting in 1924 when the National Union of

General Workers merged with the Municipal Employees Association to form a new union, the National Union of General and Municipal Workers. In 1982, following a merger with the Boilermakers and others, it became the General, Municipal Boilermakers and Allied Trade Unions – being known more snappily since then by its initials, the GMB. Today it has over 600,000 members, many of them manual workers, council workers and care workers.

Carr's at the time when Ann joined in 1991 was not a closed shop – which it had been when Barbara joined in 1977 – but when new people joined the firm, a union rep was allowed to talk to each one and explain the benefits of the union.

Ann still worked full-time on the Bourbon line, but was allowed roughly half an hour a week for union duties, as long as she notified her charge hand well in advance. She had to attend meetings with the other shop stewards and then report back to her section any excitements, such as pay negotiations or better hours, or to distribute leaflets. Being a shop steward was not very arduous, and attracted no more pay. She did the same packing work, remained on the same wages, paid by Carr's, but she felt it was worthwhile.

'When I first joined Carr's, health and safety issues were still fairly lax. Girls supposedly had always to have their hair tucked under their caps, but many pushed their cap back to expose their fringe, or let bits hang out. They wore jewellery when they were not supposed to. They were allowed to wear anything or their feet, like sandals or flip-flops, which was so dangerous. There were a lot of accidents – people tripping, falling over. The work-place was very congested and old-fashioned with lots of metal steps and piles of pallets left lying around.'

The union, according to Ann, was very supportive of all the new health and safety measures when they came in, though many of the girls didn't like them. Some moaned about the safety shoes when they were introduced, which from then on they all had to wear. Many complained that the shoes, black and rather lumpy and heavy, like policemen's shoes, looked awful and that they hurt their feet.

After a year or so as a shop steward, still working on the Bourbon line, Ann was asked to become convenor. This meant working with all the shop stewards in the factory, the first woman at Carr's to have that position. She now had her own little office and did the job full-time, but Carr's still paid her wages, under a union agreement.

She now had to attended regular national meetings of other convenors in the McVitie section of United Biscuits – which now consisted of biscuit factories in Harlesden in London, Tollcross in Glasgow, Ashby de la Zouch in Leicestershire, in Manchester and Carlisle.

She was expected at these meetings to convey what was happening at the Carlisle factory, then come back and tell the ten Carr's shop stewards the latest on any group negotiations or developments with the main United Biscuits management. Their headquarters was at Hayes in London.

A lot of her time as the factory convenor was spent on discipline problems at the Carr's factory. When the management gave warnings and suspensions, the third of which usually ended in the sack, it was the job of Ann and the other shop stewards to find out what had happened and defend the offender, if appropriate. They would represent the workforce in such disputes – as long as they were paid-up members of the union.

'We had to be honest with them. If we looked at their record, and heard both sides of what had happened, we would often have to say they were likely to end up with a warning. Most of the discipline problems we dealt with were to do with absence.

'A lot of the girls would whine and would often say, "I hate it here." But of course they didn't leave. They knew they were well paid and wouldn't get a better job anywhere else in Carlisle. That's why Carr's has always had so many long-service workers, who stay for decades.'

There were occasionally more serious discipline problems than staying on the sick too long. Such as fights. One fight involved two women who had been arguing over another woman. They were both sent home. In the subsequent investigation, the factory manager at the time listened to their defence, then said that's it, you are both sacked.

'There were always lots of difficulties when the summer holidays came, as there always is in factories with a lot of women. Women with children have such trouble getting cover in the long summer holidays.

'They would come to the shop stewards and say could they have a different shift for the summer, and we would say yes, if they could get a swap.'

There was never a strike in Ann's time as convenor at the Carr's factory – or before or after, as far as she was aware – but she says they got near it a few times. Action would be threatened, then, as the deadline approached, an agreement would be reached.

'The arguments were usually over pay and conditions, the usual problems in any factory or workplace. We wanted pay to be linked to inflation and they would say no, they couldn't afford it and would refuse. Then we would dig in our heels. Or it would be about shifts. They always caused a lot of complaints, with workers insisting their shifts were unfair and unreasonable, and saying if they had to do them they should be better paid. The company would say no. So it went on, but we never actually downed tools.

'It was challenging at times, but we always thought we had a good working relationship with the local management...'

Chapter 16
Ivy

In the 1980s, Ivy was offered another promotion. Unlike Barbara, she was never ambitious. It just seemed to happen. So she says. She never asked or applied.

With being there so long, knowing how everything worked, she seemed a suitable person to be given a bit more responsibility. Especially as she was still unmarried, and so could be more flexible than many of the married women or those with children.

Her work as a trainer of the new girls had clearly gone so well, Ivy being such a comforting, understanding soul, always with a joke or a laugh.

At the age of fifty-three, Ivy decided that she should learn to drive. Being a single woman living at home, she didn't have any children to support or many house bills, so felt she could afford the lessons.

'I loved going out in the car with my instructor. But I failed twice, which was disappointing, even though I had spent every spare moment reading the Highway Code.

'But I passed the third time – and felt on top of the world. When I got into work they all congratulated me.

'I decided to buy my own car, even though I knew people would be jealous of me, which they were. I could not have been happier. It felt amazing. Now I could go wherever I wanted to.'

The car she bought was a second-hand Triumph Herald, red and white, which cost her £250.

Ivy's little car was smart for Carlisle, and rather jaunty for a single working girl in her fifties.

It came in very useful when out of the blue she was offered a new job – working in personnel.

It was not an office job, as such, more of a going out of the office job, leaving the factory to go and see workers in their homes, or visiting the sick in hospital, acting as a sort of factory social worker. Many of the workers knew her by then, as an old hand of over thirty-five years, and a long-time charge hand. And she knew them, and understood the sort of work they had been doing.

'One day I had to go and see this woman who had taken a funny turn at work and been sent home. She lived in Cumwhinton, a village out in the country, in this lovely cottage with roses by the door and a pretty garden. I knocked at the door and she appeared. I asked her how she was and said much better, thanks.

'She then shouted for her sister, she was living with her, and I got invited in. They set the table with their best tablecloth and got out the best china and gave me tea and cakes and scones.

'We were sitting at their little front window, looking out at the garden, chatting away, having tea and scones, and I remember thinking to myself "This is it really, Ivy. How can anything be nicer than this? If they could see me now, back at the factory!"

'I felt so lucky to have such a nice job. It had been hard, mind, for many years, physically hard, but now it wasn't hard any more. It was all pleasure, getting out and meeting people – and having tea and scones!'

One of her jobs in personnel was to represent the company at the funerals of ex-workers. Sometimes she found herself doing two or three funerals a day, leaving the crematorium door, then turning round and going in again for the next funeral.

Not long after she had joined the personnel department, she was directed one day by the medical department to visit a sick worker, to check on his condition. 'And I was also told to bring back one of his stools. I thought that was queer and funny, but I did what I was told to do. I picked up one of his kitchen stools and took it back in my car and presented it to the factory nurse. I never heard the end of that. I had never heard the expression "stools" before. I was told to say nothing, but to go back and return the kitchen stool at once.'

Working in personnel led to one of the big excitements in her life – her first aeroplane flight. This happened in the late 1980s, by which time she was approaching sixty but had still not been abroad or flown in a plane.

Once United Biscuits had taken over the factory, the ceremonies that were put on for long-serving staff where they would be honoured for all their good work no longer took place in Carlisle, as in the old days of the Carr family when one of the Carrs would personally hand over a long-service award and their photograph would appear in the *Topper Off*. Now they were part of a large group with its headquarters three hundred miles away in London.

'I was given the job of accompanying a couple of long-service workers down to London. I drove them across to Newcastle, got the plane to London, and then went to the headquarters. That first time we went, I was too scared about the thought of London that I decided to do it all in one day. We could all have stayed overnight in a hotel, the company would have paid for it, but I was nervous.

'I got in a queer panic one time. When we got to London, they sent a chauffeur, but he had been given the wrong directions and we got lost, which wasn't my fault. When we got there, the Chairman of United Biscuits was standing outside waiting for us. I felt terrible.'

By 1990, still working in personnel, Ivy had notched up over forty years since she had started working in Carr's just after the war. Those forty-odd years had seen huge changes in the ownership of Carr's, with the end of the Carr's family connections and then two takeovers. Control of the factory had moved to United Biscuit's corporate headquarters in Hayes, west London.

There had also been huge changes in the nature and organisation of the biscuit industry as a whole – on what we were eating, on who was producing it and where.

Competition had always been intense, long before any takeovers or amalgamations, right from the early beginnings in the nineteenth century, with all the well-known brands, like Carr's, McVitie's, Crawford's, Huntley & Palmers being deadly rivals. Their salesmen, out in the country at large, and then the world, would try to outdo each other with special offers and promotions, offering discounts if you took a certain number of biscuits, or give you a special mahogany and glass showcase to put on your shop counter.

Grocery stores would be visited twice a week, so grocery owners had to be quick to fill up their free Carr's or Crawford's showcase with the correct brand, till the salesman had gone. In London in 1900, the Meredith & Drew salesman used to boast that an order posted before midnight would be delivered the next day anywhere in the London area. This was at a time when there were up to five postal deliveries a day.

The rival companies, desperate to get extra orders, targeted all the local grocery shops whenever they had a special promotion, handing out samples, posters, displays and other inducements. So many of the gimmicks and sales promotions, advertising and offers, which we think now are terribly modern, were all being done well over a hundred years ago.

Even after many of the major brands combined – as McVitie's and Price and McFarlane Lang did in 1948 to mark the start of United Biscuits, joined by Carr's in 1972 – the rivalry remained fierce, knowing that failure or falling behind, even temporarily, would have the accountants and investment bankers deciding to pull out, selling off any half-decent assets or closing down the unprofitable factories.

In the past, almost all the long-established biscuit firms, with their well-known names, had been family created and run, with grandchildren and great-grandchildren, like the Carrs and the Langs and the Crawfords, continuing to be involved in the family firm or the biscuit world until well into the 1960s and 1970s.

Family businesses, on the whole, tend to think about the future as much as the present, planning for con-tinuity and continuation rather than short-term gains. They are concerned about the welfare of the workers more than feeding the shareholders. Profits tend to be ploughed back into the firm, not into dividends.

There was a moral element to many of those founding families. A lot of them, like the Carrs, were

Quakers, who tried to create model conditions for their workers, promote their health and spiritual needs and improve their housing, as well as their pay packets. The Scottish biscuit families, while not Quakers, were often God-fearing and kirk-going.

And yet at the same time, those long-lasting biscuit dynasties seemed to have been able to produce enterprising and entrepreneurial figures in every generation, if not in the direct descendants then among cousins and second cousins. Theodore Carr, for example, was just as keen on harnessing and developing the latest inventions and methods as his grandfather J.D. had been. When it's your family firm, you can act quickly, even sometimes just on a whim, without having to worry too much about meetings or market research.

After the 1970s, once the biscuit firms found themselves part of groups, and then later when companies went global, it became nearly impossible to work out who exactly owned which brand, which product and where exactly they operated from. And of course the fear always was, in a faraway place like Carlisle, that the decision makers would have no personal knowledge or little personal interest in a little local factory that made Table Water Biscuits.

And yet these long-established family firms – with the same families working in them over the decades, not just the same families owning them – had survived two world wars, adjusting to the new conditions, aiding the war effort as much as they could and helping their workers survive.

With the arrival of the big groups, and lots of factories under the same umbrella, it was vital to have some sort of edge, some sort of speciality. The mass-selling, popular biscuits, such as custard creams and Bourbons, could be spread around, made anywhere, all to the same format, the same packaging, so you didn't know where they originated.

Carr's of Carlisle were fortunate that they had built up such a reputation with their Table Water Biscuits. But they too were affected by changes in taste over the years, with new variations coming, such as the garlic water biscuits that Dorothy had found created such a smell.

Rich, sugary biscuits had always been the mainstay of the trade in the nineteenth and early twentieth centuries, and remained so, but tastes did change with people wanting lighter, crispier, healthier biscuits. Cheese sandwich biscuits became very popular in the pre-war years, with firms boasting that they were using the best possible, tastiest, spreadiest cheese. 'A Meal for a Penny', was a slogan that lasted for many years.

One of the big rivals to biscuits, sweet or savoury, which scared the hell out of many of the biscuit men, was the rise of crisps. The origins are vague and disputed, but frying thin slices of potato had been around in some form for centuries. American legend has it that 'potato chips', as they're called there, were invented in Saratoga Springs in 1853.

In the UK, we appear to have taken the idea of crisps from France rather than the USA. In 1909, a London merchant grocer on holiday in Paris noticed a street vendor outside a Paris theatre doing a good trade in 'perles de Paris', which turned out to be potato wafers which he fried in oil. He bought the vendor over to London, got him to explain his methods, and set about working out a way of creating crisps on a larger scale. Eventually, Meredith & Drew took over his crisp business and expanded it. So early on, the biscuit makers did have a stake in crisps, which was just as well for their continued survival.

The biggest crisp makers in the UK became Smiths, founded in Cricklewood in 1920, famous for their invention of inserting a little twist of salt in a grease-proof piece of blue paper into each bag of crisps. (Smiths were later subsumed into Walkers, today's biggest UK maker of crisps.) After simple salted crisps came all the variations on a theme, with cheese and onion and barbecue flavours, plus dozens of other flavours, some highly unlikely.

Packets of nuts and raisins also had great success, providing more competition for biscuits. As with crisps in the early decades, their sales were mainly through licensed premises, that is, in pubs. In the post-war years in the UK, crisps and nuts were about the only edible items you could buy in most pubs.

One of the attractions for United Biscuits when they took over Meredith & Drew in 1966 was to get access to their crisp production and sales. Two years later, in 1968, they also took over KP Nuts. The name comes from Kenyon Produce, an ancient jams and pickles firm in Rotherham, founded in 1853, who turned to peanuts in 1953. By this time, crisps and savoury snacks were becoming huge business, just as biscuits had been a hundred years earlier.

The other big threat and worry for the biscuit world was the rise of the supermarkets. From the 1960s onwards, they were springing up in most towns, if not quite as quickly in Carlisle as elsewhere. The main threat that supermarkets posed was the creation of own-brand products. Marks & Spencer was about the first, with their St Michael label.

Many of the traditional biscuit firms refused to manufacture own-brand biscuits at first, being proud of their own long-established names, but with over-production in the biscuit world, several factories realised it was an easy way to get steady bulk orders. It also saved on their advertising budgets. Once own brand became common, the supermarkets were able to beat down the manufacturers on price, making their profit margins thinner and thinner.

Increased interest in healthy eating has created a market for low-calorie snacks, prompting manufacturers to create new dry crispbread biscuits, and the nation's growing taste for Indian or Thai foods has ensured that biscuit manufacturers always have to be on their toes.

Such changes and developments, competition and trends in the industry, and in the national habits as a whole, did not worry our six biscuit girls unduly, as they worked away in the Carr's factory. Their normal working day went on much as before.

New lines did of course regularly come in, but the process of packing them continued, with only minimal improvements in the systems, as automatic machines which might save them labour were usually too expensive to install.

Occasionally when they went home after a day's shift there might be the odd comment about a new aroma lingering in the air, picked up from the new and exciting product or ingredient which had been added to Carr's traditional range, such as curry-flavoured water biscuits. Both Jonathan Dodgson and Theodore would doubtless have welcomed such innovations. They were always on the lookout for new lines, new temptations.

In the case of Ivy, having finished on the production lines, now shepherding pensioners to get their deserved long-service awards, she was not too bothered by all the changes. After all these years she felt she had done her bit.

In 1993, Ivy herself had the honour of receiving a long-service presentation at the United Biscuits headquarters. It was a compulsory retirement, having reached the age of sixty. She had completed forty-five years of continuous service – apart from nine months off when she had cared for her dying mother.

Ivy receives her award for 45 years of long service in 1993, aged 60

Chapter 17
Dulcie

Dulcie in 2013

Dulcie, Dorothy and Jean, the other three women who, like Ivy, had been born pre-war, were also soon coming up to their sixtieth birthdays, although none of them had been there as long or as continuously as Ivy. They had had breaks for various reasons, such as marriages and children, or been employed elsewhere for a period of time.

Dulcie, the one who had been married twice and had the daughter with hearing problems, had begun to suffer from back and shoulder pains in her fifties, plus the dreaded bakehouse legs.

In 1998, aged fifty-nine, she decided to retire. She had done almost thirty years at Carr's – five as a teenage messenger girl – then later she did twenty-four consecutive years. They included a couple of short spells as a timekeeper and as a clerk in the office, but mostly she had been working on the line, packing crackers. She felt her body had had enough.

She and her husband Bob were still living in the old farmhouse about ten miles from Carlisle which they had bought many years ago in the sixties and had managed, eventually, to convert most of it.

But then in 2002 her husband Bob died. Heart problems had forced him to retire prematurely from work, and then he developed pancreatic cancer.

Fortunately, her daughters came to live either side of Dulcie, in converted barns that had been part of the old farmhouse. But Dulcie had never passed her driving test. So when Bob died, she was left without a car, deep in the country.

'I had thought a few times over the years about learning to drive, but just sitting in a car at the driving wheel made me nervous.'

Both Elizabeth and Louise could drive, so they were able to help take their mum to town when necessary or to bingo.

Dulcie went on to enjoy some exciting holidays since becoming a widow, often with her daughters and grandchildren or with friends. She has been on two cruises – one to the Mediterranean and one to the Caribbean – and has photographs to prove it, of her laughing and joking with the captain.

On holiday in Egypt in 2011 she found her back was giving her discomfort. She had been taking paracetamol for some time, but it didn't seem to be helping any more. 'I was going up these steps from the dining room and the pain was suddenly agonising, the worst ever. When I got home, I went to see the doctor. He gave me more pain-killers, then did an X-ray which showed nothing. But the pain was getting worse so he put me on morphine.

'Eventually I was sent to the RVI in Newcastle. A scan showed malignant tumours on my spine. They operated and I was in for two weeks. Then I had a week of radiotherapy. That was horrible. It made me feel sick all the time.'

Two years later, she was down to a check-up every three months and felt fine, though she had recently been put on steroid tablets, not for the pain, but to help build her up. She was walking with a stick, but was otherwise fit and as lively as ever and even swearing now and again, as she did in her heyday on the line at Carr's, especially when protecting her daughter. She had no computer but managed to acquire a mobile phone, though hadn't quite mastered it.

She keeps up with popular music, listening to CFM, the local commercial station. 'My grandchildren are always amazed that I know the latest songs.'

Dulcie has little interest in politics, but she always votes, just as mother always voted. 'Mind you, I never knew how she voted. I vote Conservative, not that I think much of politicians these days. I quite admired Mrs Thatcher. J.F. Kennedy, I did like him. I felt safe when he was alive.'

She cooked for her girls when they were growing up, and her husband, making much the same sort of meals that her mother did, but today does no cooking. 'It's my legs. I can't stand. The most I ever do is beans on toast. I rely today on Elizabeth to do some cooking for me.'

She usually has biscuits in the house for visitors, and herself, and still enjoys chocolate biscuits best, wishing that Carr's Sports biscuits had never been discontinued. They were her favourite.

Sports biscuits were a bit like Penguin, a chocolate-coated biscuit bar, which in the post-war years were immensely popular. Sports sold well for Carr's and were heavily promoted, with lots of associated merchandising and souvenirs, such as special tins and sets of cards showing footballers. In their wisdom, United Biscuits appeared to think that there were too many other similar chocolate bars, such as Lunch and also Club, produced by Jacob's, also now in the United Biscuits empire.

Penguin, the brand leader, was created in 1932 by William McDonald of Glasgow and in the long history of biscuit creations, its birth was unusual. Most of our classic biscuits were first produced by well-known biscuit manufacturers, usually family firms, but William McDonald was a salesmen, on his own, working in the biscuit trade. One of his specialities was importing foreign biscuits, then selling them on to the trade.

When he hit upon the idea of coating biscuits in chocolate, which had not been done before, he put up his own money to open a factory. His early versions were round in shape, till he hit on an oblong cream-filled biscuit, coated with chocolate. It was only after the war in conjunction with an advertising agency, Colman, Prentis and Varley, that they were given the name Penguin.

From then on, they were promoted purely on their name – with the product being pushed, not the firm, which again was unusual in the biscuit world. We still today think of Carr's Water Biscuits or Jacob's Cream Crackers whereas Penguin, well, it's just a Penguin, who knows who produces them? Today it is in fact United Biscuits, under the McVitie's name. Little wonder Sports biscuits eventually disappeared from the Carr's portfolio, much to Dulcie's regret.

'When I worked there, I liked all their biscuits, they were all good. Yes, we were not supposed to eat any while we were working, but we did, discreetly. I never cared for the fig rolls, which I know some of the girls loved. I was very fond of custard creams and whole-meal digestives, the ones half-coated with chocolate.

'In my day, the staff could still get so called cheap biscuits at the factory shop, but in the end, they weren't all that much cheaper. I used to find Littlewoods sometimes did cheaper ones. We did get a box of chocolates at Christmas, but not every Christmas.'

Looking back on her life, she regretted two things – not learning to drive and being so awful to her mum when she was young with her wild, impetuous love life. 'I can't bear to think what I put her through.'

In the end she had a long and happy marriage to Bob. 'As happy as marriages can be...'

Workwise, she had no regret about all the years spent at Carr's, and didn't think that with her talents and education she should have tried harder to get and retain an office job rather than spending so much time in unskilled work on a factory floor.

'The factory girls were terrific. I have nothing against them. I made some great friends, which I still have.

'But to be honest, I did it for the money. The money was always good for Carlisle and was the main reason for staying all those years. But I still enjoyed it, otherwise I would have left.'

On the whole, she considered she had a happy life. 'I've always been a happy sort of person. I suppose the only bad time was when we discovered Louise was deaf, and then when she had to go off to that special school. That was hard.

'I don't like being ill and not being able to do much, but my nature is not to worry about the future, just take each day as it comes. I'm lucky having Elizabeth. I don't know how I would have survived, living out here and not being so well, without her. She is my rock. So I'm happy in that sense, as happy as I can be.'

She thought about getting a tattoo. It's the sort of daft thing she used to do many years ago when she was younger, she says, but her poor health distracted her in the last few years from too many wild indulgences.

'I remember when I worked at Carr's, I suppose I must have been in my thirties, going out with my girlfriends dressed as scrubbers and the next evening dressed as flappers. I once shaved my hair, right up the back, not at the front. Can't remember why or what the style was called.

'I've just got these false nails, nice, aren't they, to make my hands look better. Me and Louise have exactly the same swelling on our index finger of our right hands – look, it's a huge lump. We both put it down to working on the line at Carr's, lifting up hot biscuits for all those years.

'Having done my nails, I think a tattoo will be next. On my shoulder or on my hand. Someone suggested the design should be a Carr's custard cream, you know, with the fern pattern. That would be funny, but I think I've had enough with Carr's. I'll probably go for something pretty, like a butterfly.'

Chapter 18
Dorothy

Dorothy in 2013

Dorothy, born like Dulcie in 1939, also retired in 1999, but her service to Carr's had not been as long as Dulcie's, nor of course Ivy's. Dorothy had had all those years after leaving her country school working in a bakery shop and then as a machinist.

But unlike Ivy and Dulcie, she had not experienced or been offered or desired any promotions or changes of job. During her twenty-two years at Carr's she had been working on the same morning shift, six to two, and in the same department, packing water biscuits.

'Towards the end of my time, I suppose in the 1990s, we had quite a few men, old men and young men, working on the line with us. No, it didn't bother me, working with men for a change. The older men tended to be good workers, better than some of the new young lasses we were getting. Older men were finding it difficult to find work at the time, so were grateful.

'I had paid all my stamps, so when I discovered when I got to fifty-nine that I would get a good pension, I decided to leave. I felt I had had enough, done enough work. I wasn't ill, I was still fit, no problems, just feeling a bit tireder. I had been working since I was fifteen. After forty-five years, I thought I had done enough.'

She was still unmarried, still living at home with her parents when she retired, though she had learned to drive by then and bought a little car.

Unlike Ivy, she did not have the problem or duty of being the grown-up daughter still at home who had to look after an ailing mother. Dorothy's mother died suddenly in 2010, aged ninety-two after heart problems, so she had little nursing or caring to do. Her father had died in 2004.

She inherited their house in Carlisle and lived there for a while, but got fed up with the parking problems.

'I was a woman on my own and always felt hemmed in. Everyone in the street now seemed to have two cars. I was always asking them, "Can you move your car?" I decided to move somewhere where I had my own garage. I had always fancied a bungalow as I would be able to clean all my own windows.

'My mum had wanted a bungalow, but my father had never wanted to move. So two years ago I bought this bungalow. No, I don't want to tell you how much or how much I got for my parents' house. That's private.'

Her bungalow is in a cul-de-sac, all very quiet. Her garden is immaculate, all done by Dorothy, just a mile to the west of the Carr's factory.

She goes swimming in the Carlisle baths twice a week, and once a week she plays bingo, going with Dulcie. She had never been particularly close to Dulcie while they worked at Carr's, as Dulcie had moved around while Dorothy stayed put, but since retirement, they have become good friends.

They go to Workington for their bingo night out, some thirty miles away from Carlisle, out on the old industrial coast, which seems a long trail, when Carlisle is well appointed with bingo halls.

'I like the bus ride there. We go on the bus, with our free bus pass. It puts in the day. We might look round the shops as well.'

Her normal expenditure on a bingo day is £10 but she is up on the year, having had a good win of £350. She spent it on new blinds for her front window.

She has never paid much attention to the changing styles and fashions, making a lot of her own clothes from patterns. 'I remember once liking the look of a Coco Chanel dress, her little black dress, but I never had one. I did wear nylons when they came in, with seams up the back, and something to keep them up, which I suppose was a girdle or perhaps suspenders. Something anyway. My mother wore a corset but I never liked the idea of them. I remember tights coming in, but I never wore them. Not sure why. I've never liked trousers, but I do have a pair and might wear them in the winter on Sunday mornings when I'm going swimming.'

As a teenager and young girl, she cut out photos of Elvis, Tommy Steele and Roy Rogers the cowboy. 'I also liked the Dave Clark Five and Freddie and the Dreamers, but I never went to any live shows. Living in the country, you couldn't really get to things like that. Modern music, well it doesn't bother me either way. It's all right I suppose, up to a point.

'We never got a daily paper either, as we were too far from a shop, but my father did buy the *Cumberland News* each week and also the *Westmorland Herald*, which was the Penrith paper.'

Today, she still does not read a daily paper, but she buys the *Cumberland News* on a Friday and on Sunday always buys the *Sunday Post* after she has been swimming. Interesting how the *Sunday Post*, an old-fashioned Scottish paper, featured in so many of the childhoods of our biscuit girls, and is still being read today.

Dorothy is not a great biscuit eater – in fact she finds she doesn't eat a lot these days since her parents died.

'When I was young, my mother made her own biscuits, and I loved them, especially her ginger biscuits. When we went to town, we would often go to Woolworths and buy a pound of mixed sweet biscuits. You could go round the tins and take a handful of each sort you fancied, till you had enough for a pound. I liked anything with jam in it, that was a treat. You didn't get many sweets during the war, so all children loved anything sweet.'

While working at Carr's, she always sampled whatever line she was working on, even though it was against the rules. 'I liked to try them all – Garibaldis, fig rolls, Morning Coffee, any sort of chocolate biscuits. I liked custard creams but I never liked Bourbons. I thought their filling was a bit dry.'

Today, she will buy the odd packet of sweet biscuits when she is shopping, if she remembers, usually digestives or shortbread, just to have them in the house for visitors. She never buys Carr's water biscuits, despite all those years spent packing them.

'Well you wouldn't would you, they are for parties, and I don't have parties. They're for putting stuff on top, stuff like cheese, to hand round. You couldn't eat them on their own. Anyway, they're a bit plain for my taste.'

Dorothy, living on her own, does all her own cooking and tries to eat regular meals, knowing she should, to keep up her strength. She does most of the plain, old-fashioned dishes which her mother made, such as hot pot. 'I usually have fish once a week as well, white fish. We didn't often have fish when I was a girl, living out in the country. I usually have it with parsley sauce. I buy it in a packet, and add milk.

'I suppose now I think about it, I do have a slightly different diet from my parents. I don't remember any sauces as a girl. Everything really was plain. I have more variety in the meals I make compared with my mother. I often make a sauce to go with whatever I'm having, which she never did. If I'm out say with my sister, which isn't very often, I will order salmon with a sauce, just to see what it tastes like.

'Once a fortnight or so I do have a Chinese takeaway. There are so many of them round here, open all the time and very reasonable. I've grown quite used to a Chinese. But I've never had Indian or Thai and I don't eat Italian or French. The idea of eating frogs' legs or octopus, ugh. I don't even like pasta.

'But I keep on meaning to try a Thai restaurant, as people say they are nice. I would have to go with someone. Well, I might order something and not like it and it would be wasted, wouldn't it? I'd need the other person to eat it up.

'I don't drink, never have done. I don't like the taste of wine. But I do usually have a bottle of rum in the house, like my mam did. I use it for making rum sauce for the Christmas pudding. That's the only way I like rum.'

She still doesn't like fried tomatoes, her one hatred as a girl, but has now added to it runny cheese. 'I mean wet cheese, you know, when they put it on the top of things, and it's all runny. I don't even like toasted cheese. What I like is dry, natural cheese.'

Dorothy has no interest in politics and doesn't vote. 'I have no idea how my parents voted. Or if they did. Politics were never discussed at home. I still don't really understand politics, but it seems to me they just think about themselves. I quite liked Mrs Thatcher. She would say no to people. The others never seem to be able to say no to anyone.'

She never read much as a girl and doesn't read books today. She never joined any library, or the Brownies or Guides. Living in the country made those sorts of activities difficult.

She goes to the Carr's pensioners club each month, where she meets Ivy, who used to be her trainer, Jean, who was at one time her charge hand, Ann, who was her union rep and Dulcie. She doesn't attend church, despite being brought up as a Methodist and having had to go to chapel every Sunday as a child.

She is fit and active, no aches and pains or frozen shoulders, unlike some of the ex-workers. Perhaps she never exactly knocked herself out? She smiles at that.

More likely her nature is to be calm and placid. By remaining for those twenty-two years at Carr's as a humble packer, with no wish for promotion to charge hand, perhaps she had avoided too much unnecessary stress. In the end, it was being tired of working, of going out to work, not physical exhaustion or pain, which made her pleased to retire.

'Standing for twenty-two years on a stone floor, that can't have been good for you, but it didn't really bother me. I never complained. Towards the end they did bring in those safety shoes, those lumpy things, that we had to wear. Some of the girls moaned. I didn't. I liked them. They felt comfy and did my feet good.'

In 1996, aged fifty-seven, she went in a plane for the first time. She had, of course, been *on* a plane aged three in 1942 when her father put her on the wing of the crashed Lancaster bomber. She went to Tunisia, invited by her sister and family to join them on their holiday. 'It was a bit worrying at first. We went from Birmingham airport and when it took off, it swung right round. It was very alarming, but it was OK in the end. I've been abroad four times since then.'

She visits the Carlisle crematorium on her parents' birthdays and on their wedding anniversary and other significant dates.

'Their ashes are in the March Garden – there's a garden for each month of the year. They were both born in March. Their names are in the memorial book inside. There's nothing on the place where I scattered their ashes. But I know the exact spot. I scattered my mother in the shade, under a tree. She always liked the shade. My father is out in the open. He always loved being out in the open.'

She misses them both, but has got used to living on her own.

'I suppose I did think I would get married, most people think they will, don't they? I had a few boyfriends, but it just didn't happen. I don't want to get married now. I feel quite happy. I like doing things my way, being my own boss. I suppose the only thing I do miss is having someone to talk to, since my parents died.

'As a girl, I was really rather shy, but not now. Sometimes I think I am too outspoken. I often speak before I've thought. I don't have rows or arguments with people but sometimes I come out with my opinion when I don't have to. I often think afterwards I should have said nowt. I think perhaps I might have upset them. But then sometimes they upset me by saying things. I suppose, thinking about it, if I had to pick on one time, the happiest period in my life was when I first started work. I had my own money and was able to go out more.

'I don't think I've had what you might call low moments. I don't ever remember being at my so-called lowest. And I don't really fret about the future, not for myself. When I think thoughts of the future I think about nuclear bombs, and what they might do to the world, so I hope they might not happen. And of course I am upset at the moment when I hear about all this fighting going on out there, in the rest of the world.

'But I do feel I have had a happy life. I enjoyed my time at Carr's. I felt proud to be working for a long-established firm, sending water biscuits all over the world.

'I have no regrets. Well, none I can think of. Well, I suppose I should have stuck in harder at school, but too late for that now.'

Chapter 19
Jean

Jean in 2013

Jean was born in Liverpool in 1936, making her just three years older than Dulcie and Dorothy. Like Dulcie, she too eventually began to suffer health problems.

In 1992, after ten years as a charge hand, and before that eleven years as an packer on the line, Jean was having more and more days off than working days, with pains all over her body, some days so severe she could hardly walk or get out of bed. And at work she often had to be sent home.

After lots of tests and endless cortisone injections, she was diagnosed with fibromyalgia – a disease causing chronic pains throughout the body. It mainly occurs in women, creating physical symptoms due to some sort of stress, and is often allied with depression. Some think the causes are genetic, others believe it is environmental, perhaps going back to childhood trauma, which of course Jean suffered from greatly with her stepmother while growing up in Liverpool, or somehow connected to her childhood polio.

She has investigated her father's side of the family to find if any grandparents or other relations suffered in the same way. None of them had. But she knows nothing about her mother's family. Her mother died when Jean was three and there was no contact with her family afterwards. So she thinks it might come from her mother's side of the family. Perhaps surprisingly, while always hating her stepmother who died several years ago, Jean has always kept in touch with her stepmother's family.

Her husband Jack – the Carlisle-born soldier she met when he was stationed in Liverpool – has his own theories. He puts it down to those twenty-two years standing on concrete at Carr's. He says that must have affected all her muscles, plus coming out in the middle of the night after eight hours in a boiling-hot factory into Carlisle's cold night air.

Jean herself thinks that could not have helped her general health, but doesn't blame Carr's for her present condition.

'But quite a few of the others lasses did have things like frozen shoulders, which must have been directly aggravated by packing the biscuits.'

While still working at Carr's, but increasingly stuck at home sick, she was visited by Ivy, then working in personnel. Ivy discussed Jean's health problems with her, and her future. Ivy eventually brought the appropriate forms for Jean to sign in order to be pensioned off early on health grounds. So in 1993, aged fifty-seven after twenty-two years at Carr's, Jean retired.

Her husband Jack, now also retired, went on to suffer from ill health and today has gall bladder problems and diabetes.

Jean herself, despite her physical condition, is bright and sharp, speaks clearly and fluently, never at a loss for names and dates, unlike Jack, whose memory is not what it was.

She still has little interest in fashion, no more than she had as a child. She makes a lot of her own clothes, as she always did for herself and her children when they were growing up, working from patterns. 'But I did wear a miniskirt at one time – a bit late in the day, as I had four children by then.'

Bing Crosby is still her favourite singer. She considers modern music to be rubbish.

She has started to write her memoirs of her life growing up in wartime Liverpool to pass on to her family. She has no computer or mobile phone but has managed over the last few years to write out in longhand about 3,000 words, taking her life up to leaving school and her first job in Liverpool. It could be the makings of a Catherine Cookson novel. But she doesn't know if she will ever finish it. She reads books, liking those written by Anna Jacobs and Katie Flynn.

She eats more biscuits today than she did in her childhood growing up in Liverpool, but then it was wartime. She always has a tin of biscuits in the house, to offer visitors, or to have one herself every afternoon, with a cuppa. She still loved Jacob's Cream Crackers as she did in her childhood, and prefers them to Carr's Table Water Biscuits: 'They are a bit dry for me, I much prefer Jacob's. But I do like Carr's Cheese Thins.'

She was unaware that Jacob's is now part of the same empire as Carr's – of United Biscuits – so she was still helping company profits.

In her day at Carr's, they were never allowed to eat any of the biscuits at work, and she never did so, even behind the line. 'But there was a time, in the seventies I think, when we used to be given tickets that we could take to the works shop and buy a tin of broken biscuits very cheaply, for a couple of pennies. My children loved them. You could also buy chocolate biscuits, like Carr's Sports, but you paid more for them. Everybody loved them. For a while we also got given a tin of biscuits at Christmas as our Christmas present, but that had stopped before I left.'

Jean does all the cooking, for herself and her husband, and has not altered her cooking and eating habits since she was young, not having much truck with what she calls modern fancy dishes and ingredients, sticking to the dishes that her grandmother made for her during the war, such as scouse and roasts.

'I had to learn to cook and bake when I left home, and lived on my own, but I just copied what I had seen my grandmother doing. In our early married life, when my husband was on evening shifts, and coming back very late, I would leave his meal for him. It could be anything, really. If it was something hot, like scouse stew, or sausages and mash, or corn beef hash, I would put it on a plate, a sort of deep oval one, like a soup bowl, and leave it on top of a pan of hot water, which I'd boiled. Then I'd put another plate on top. It did keep the food hot, or at least warm, for quite a long time. It was safe and cheap and if he didn't come home till late, it didn't get burned or waste gas. Mind you, it might have gone cold, but that was his problem.

'Today our habits have not changed since we were first married. We still prefer the old types of food. As for shopping, I just go to wherever is the cheapest. We never have drink in the house.'

Neither Jean nor her husband votes, though growing up in Liverpool she came from a strong Liberal home. 'In those days, the Liberals were the top party in Liverpool.

'I didn't like Tony Blair, right from the beginning. Margaret Thatcher was all right, I suppose. But really I think they are all the same. They promise heaven on earth – but you always end with prices going sky high.'

Because of their health, her and her husband's social life has become restricted, but they still have a little car, for which they get disability benefits. Neither of them has ever been abroad or flown in a plane – though Jean did sit in a plane once, while in the WAAF. Their holidays have been spent in England, usually in a caravan in Lincolnshire.

Their four children have produced ten grand-children and eight great-grandchildren. There have alas been some bad times and worries with one member of her family – and they have not spoken for two years.

Has it been a happy life? Jean thought long and decided it had been hard rather than happy. She was happy at Carr's, no complaints there, the best thing being the other lasses, but if she had her life over again, she would have liked more money. She always seemed to have money problems.

'I suppose the happiest time in my life, which might seem strange now, was during the war. You got four rides for a penny on the tram and we would go to places like Woolton Woods near Speke Airport, which is now called John Lennon Airport. For tuppence you could go across on the ferry to New Brighton. You can't travel anywhere for those prices any more. We also used to go to Southport. So even though there was a war on, and rationing for many years later, when I look back, all I remember is the fun we used to have.

'I also enjoyed being a teenager. You had no worries, no commitments to other people, no husband or children. You could just please yourself. As a teenager I got a bit rebellious, going off to live on my own. I suppose it was to do with my mother dying when I was a baby and my dad away in the war. But I don't feel rebellious any more. I've changed a lot. If anything, I've gone a bit too soft.

'I do worry about the future, about whether I will be able to cope or not. My hands are now going, so I can't write as well as I used to. That's my latest worry.

'Overall, thinking about it now, I suppose what I feel is that I have not achieved much in life, not as much as I would have liked.'

However, they did manage to buy their council house – paying £6,000 for it in 1983, but then had trouble paying the mortgage and lost the house for a few years. They were allowed to rent it for a while, then finally bought it back again.

'I have thought about leaving him several times, as many wives do. He drove me mad at times and I wanted to walk out of the door. I was just fed up with him. Nothing specific. Just like many wives, I suppose.'

Jack, meanwhile is sitting by the gas fire, filling in a puzzle book, smiling to himself, not at all upset by what his wife is saying.

'But we stuck it out together. And now it's coming up soon for sixty years married. There seems no point in leaving him now, or leaving Carlisle, even if I could, or even if I really wanted to. Not after all this time.'

Chapter 20
Barbara

Barbara in 2013

As post-war children, Ann and Barbara – born in 1949 1953 respectively – had opportunities that became available to women today which were denied those in previous generations, but went on to experience some of our modern post-war pleasures and problems. Could it be because women expect more today, demand more today than their sisters brought up in those tough wartime years?

Both Barbara and Ann, for example, are whizzes on their computer and dab hands on their mobile phones, unlike our four women born in the 1930s. Having started as packers on the line, they each progressed at work, though in different ways, and also invested in property. Especially Barbara.

In 2002 after fifteen years or so as a charge hand/supervisor, Barbara became a manager, gaining quite an increase in her salary – going from £16,000 to £22,000. She was now working inside an office, not being able to help out on the lines as frequently as she had done as a supervisor. But she still tried to spend as much time as possible on the factory floor, where she could see what was actually going on in the areas she was responsible for.

She was technically a section leader, responsible for several of the plants – as the main biscuit production and packing areas are called – with around a hundred workers under her supervision. She had to ensure all the lines were running safely, reduce waste, think about health and safety.

'My shoulders, arms and wrists had begun to ache all the time by then, once I got to around fifty, which happens to so many of the girls. On a good day, you may hardly feel it, but on a bad day you can hardly get out of bed, far less face going into work. So, I felt it was time to do less physical work and jumped at the management job when it came up.'

One of the problems Barbara had to face as a manager was the Carlisle floods of 2005. In the early part of the twenty-first century, there did seem to be an unusual spate of floods all over the country, which might have been somehow connected with global warming, a threat that Ivy and anyone else born in the 1930s tend not to worry about as much as the next generation.

On 7 January 2005, there had been unusually heavy rain over the Lake District hills and the Pennines – a month's worth of rain falling in just twenty-four hours. Carlisle happens to be at the confluence of three rivers: the river Eden, the main river, is joined in Carlisle by two smaller ones, the Caldew and the Petteril. The city has often experienced floods over the centuries, but this was said to be the worst since the 1830s – the decade when J.D. Carr opened his biscuit factory in Caldewgate.

The next day, 8 January, over 1,800 homes were flooded in the city and had to be abandoned, with another 1,000 homes in the surrounding villages and smaller towns and countryside equally affected. Sewers and drains could not cope, nor could the normal flood barriers. Three people were killed, and the total damage was put at £400 million. In the city both the police station and fire station were flooded. At Brunton Park, home of Carlisle United, the pitch was six feet underwater, reaching up to the cross bars, with goldfish swimming around on the centre circle. They had escaped when the floodwaters had rushed through houses in the surrounding Warwick Road.

Carr's factory was affected immediately, being so near the Caldew and also the Eden. The whole of the ground floor was flooded, with the water up to six feet high, and had to be abandoned. Outside the main gates, cars were totally submerged and emergency services in boats rescued people from upstairs windows and roofs.

Two years later, there were 120 homes still un-occupied, especially in the Warwick Road area, but miraculously the Carr's factory was back in operation in just three months.

Barbara and other members of the management staff worked full-time, as did many of the ordinary workers, to clear up the mess. Very soon afterwards H plant, where the custard creams and Bourbons were made, was in full operation, with three million custard creams coming off the conveyor belts every twenty-four hours.

Meanwhile, thanks to her promotions, Barbara and her husband continued to move up the property ladder. Their Link house – the first house they had bought for £11,600 – was sold for £19,000. Then they bought a semi for £21,000. In turn this was sold, for £53,000, and they paid £72,000 for a brand-new three-bedroom detached bungalow with two bathrooms and a garage. They added a conservatory and another garage, as by this time David had two cars.

'Yes, we had done quite well, coming from a council house, but it was all our own hard work. You often see people with nice houses and a big car but very often the car belongs to the company and the house is rented. You never know.'

Barbara was making the most of the explosion in property prices that was happening all over England from the seventies onwards, with prices almost everywhere doubling every five years or so and people on the property ladder becoming notionally wealthier. Carlisle prices have never been anything like those in London and the south – usually about half – or in the posh parts of the north, such as Cheshire, but values did rise steadily if not spectacularly.

If Barbara and her husband had been earning two wages in London over the same period and had used it as astutely to buy their first property in 1974, then traded up every few years, selling for at least 50 per cent more each time, taking on a bigger mortgage and a better house in a better area – then over the thirty years, by the year 2004, they could well have ended up as millionaires. Perhaps even £2 million by 2014. At least on paper and if they had lived and bought in London. By Carlisle standards, though, they had done very well.

In 2006, while stretching in bed one day, Barbara happened to touch her right breast. She immediately realised she could not quite feel it. 'It felt numb, the way your jaw feels after you had a filling at the dentist and the anaesthetic has not quite worn off. You can feel it – but not feel it. But there was no lump, so I wasn't too worried.'

She waited two months before seeing a doctor. He gave her some painkillers at first, not quite sure what the problem was, then told her he had made a hospital appointment for her at 8.30 on the following Wednesday morning.

Her starting hour at Carr's was still six in the morning, so she went to work first, then slipped out to the hospital after letting her senior department manager know, telling him she shouldn't be long. One of the perks of being a manager was she could leave the factory without anyone asking too many questions.

She was still at the hospital at 12.30.

'How long is this going to take?' she asked the doctors. 'I have to be back at work. I can't hang around.'

She ended up having a biopsy, which was sent off to Newcastle to be examined. Carlisle does not have sufficient equipment for such procedures – in fact, anyone with cancer in Cumbria has the extra stress of a long tiring journey for treatment to either Newcastle or Lancaster.

The result eventually came back. She was told her cancer was Grade 3 and she had to have surgery, a lumpectomy, followed by treatment.

'I told my manager what was going to happen and that I would be taking some time off. And I told him the reasons why, but I warned him that I didn't want anyone else in the factory to know. If it gets out, so I told him, I would know it was him. He did keep it secret.

'I didn't want to be walking round the factory with people thinking, "there goes Barbara the cancer sufferer" instead of, "there goes Barbara, the section leader".'

Afterwards she had chemotherapy for eighteen weeks followed by radiotherapy every day for fifteen days.

'The worst part was losing all my hair. No, now I think about it, really the worst part of all was not being in control. I felt like a failure, feeling like you were in some way letting people down by not being able to do exactly what everyone had previously relied upon you to do. I hated that. I've tried always in life to be in control. But sometimes you can't be.

'When the doctors gave me the choice of surgery or not, I hated that. They are the doctors. Not us. How can you decide? They have to be in control. But they try to pass the buck, which I can understand.'

After nine months, she was back at work, although still having to have check-ups every three months. 'I wanted to work, to get back to normal life.'

For the next two years, her job was very much the same, but then by 2008 the factory had to face the problems that the whole country was facing. The economy went into a downturn and the recession was taking hold.

296 | THE BISCUIT GIRLS

Budgets were cut, staff restructured or made redundant, economies had to be made. Staff were paid off, but Barbara was kept on and she found herself being given extra responsibilities and more plants to look after.

'There were the usual rumours about the factory closing, venture capitalists buying the company to strip all the assets. But you just live with that. We would hear one day that the McVitie factory in Scotland was closing, or the Liverpool one, so you wondered if it was true and if we would be next.

'I like to think that our loyal workforce was a factor in our continuing survival. Another theory was that our water biscuits can only be made here because of the artesian well under the factory, supplying our water. But that could be a fantasy.

'I think our situation helped us survive, our strategic position. With United Biscuits having factories in Scotland and Liverpool, we were in quite a good position, halfway between them, and also right on the motorway. But who knows all the reasons why we have somehow managed to continue here in Carlisle in this very old factory for all these long years.'

The special water theory is alas fantasy, though perhaps back in 1837 they did use a local well. Today, and for the last century or so, the factory has used normal tap water. The lack of strikes must have been an element, but the main reason for continuity was the prosaic one – the McVitie's Carlisle factory, home of Carr's, home of biscuits, was still running at a profit. Thanks, of course, to the hard work of the workers and of the management.

But the cuts did continue, to save time or money or staff, and more jobs got restructured. 'There were endless changes – and it all seemed to filter down to us, at management level.'

At the time of the 2005 floods, Barbara was responsible for the smooth running of five plants, custard creams, Bourbon creams, butter puffs, Morning Coffee and fig rolls with approximately 120 workers under her control.

Post-flood, from 2008 to 2009, Barbara was manager of the chocolate room, a cookie plant and a cracker line, and although there were now not as many staff she had to learn a new set of skills as she had not worked in the chocolate room before.

Her salary – not wages any more, once she had become management – was £30,000 a year. Her husband David, still working as a forklift driver, was on £19,000.

She finally decided she had had enough. There were more important things in life than work. It was all becoming too hard, too stressful. It was time for herself. She worked out the optimum time to go, making sure she had reached well over the thirty-year mark, to get the best financial advantage.

In June 2009, aged fifty-five, Barbara retired on roughly half pay, after thirty-two years at Carr's. Most of that time she had been involved with actually packing the biscuits, having risen from the very bottom as a packer on the line to management, one of the few female workers in 172 years to have done so well.

Today, aged sixty, Barbara looks fit and healthy. Seven years after her cancer operation, and regular series of three-monthly and then six-monthly cancer checks, she had the previous Tuesday just been pronounced 'discharged'. You are never totally clear of course, but that is about the best you can be told.

Despite her forty years of property successes, continually climbing the ladder, she was that day technically homeless. She and her husband David – still working as a forklift driver – were living in a small bedroom at the Swallow Hilltop Hotel in Carlisle. They had sold their bungalow for around three times what they had paid – three beds, two baths, two garages – and it had proved their best investment so far. The house they thought they had bought had fallen through, hence they were camping in a hotel while house-hunting again. This time they wanted a smaller, cheaper house, not trading up as in the past. That should leave them with a good nest egg for their retirement years, on which to enjoy themselves.

'We plan to be SKI parents – spending the kids' inheritance. After all, we have worked for it. But there should be enough left for them.

'I have three grandchildren. Meghan is fourteen and is a very clever and self-assured young lady. Niall is twelve and loves sport and bikes, he plays squash really quite well. The youngest addition to the family is Brooke, she is only ffiteen months old and is full of fun, with a healthy dash of mischief. I see them all regularly but tend to see more of Brooke at the moment as Meghan and Niall are at school all day and after school they are off doing their own thing with their mates.'

They had thought of moving abroad, to Tenerife, where they usually holiday twice a year, but would miss their two children and three grandchildren.

'It would also probably mean paying for them to come out every time they visit us, which of course we would do. At the moment, it would probably be too expensive for them.'

Barbara has not much interest in politics today and doesn't always vote, but would probably vote Conservative or for a coalition.

'I believe my parents voted Labour, but I would not be surprised if my mother maybe voted Conservative some of the time. In general I think politicians have a self-agenda dressed up as being for the good of the country and its people. Basically, I think a huge percentage of them are in it for themselves and have no real idea how ordinary people live. While I disagreed with a lot of Mrs Thatcher's policies, I do think she had great strength of character and made an enduring impact on the face of twentieth-century politics.'

Despite being a lady of leisure, like many people today she no longer gets a daily national paper delivered, as she did in her youth when her father had the *Daily Express*. But she does read the local papers, the *Evening News* and the *Cumberland News* on Fridays. She likes to do crosswords and sudoku puzzles.

'I always enjoyed novels by the likes of Catherine Cookson, Danielle Steele, Maeve Binchy, that type of thing. I am still a member of the local library and used to borrow books many years ago, but now I just tend to buy those that I want. Today I still read, the same type of novel really. I like books by Rebecca Forster, Rod Hoisington, Kathleen Morgan, Kristie Cook and Barbara Freethy.'

Now her two children have grown up and left home, she doesn't do as much cooking as she used to.

'When I was younger, and the children were at home, I tended to cook pretty much the same sort of things that I was used to at home, when I myself was growing up.

'At the weekend we would have the traditional Sunday roast and often had the leftovers on the Monday or I would use the stock from the meat or chicken and any leftover veg to make soup. I also used to bake fruit plate cakes and buns, jam tarts, etc. Trouble is they always went too fast 'cos when you smelled the baking, it just made you want to eat it. I also used to bake savoury pies likes bacon and egg quiche and meat pasties.

'Today I still cook things like shepherd's pie and quiche but also like to make a chicken curry or chow mein. We also like fresh fish, maybe with new potatoes and a bit of salad.

'I rarely bake cakes any more and I rarely make a "Sunday" roast, maybe once a month or so. But it could be on any day of the week, in fact hardly ever on a Sunday, as we like to go out on a Sunday to the Lake District, maybe to Keswick or Ambleside. I really don't cook very much at all at the weekend as we eat lunch out almost every Saturday as well.

'Unlike in my parents' day there is usually some kind of alcohol in the house – mainly beer and brandy and a few extras around Christmas time. I don't drink wine as is disagrees with me, but very occasionally I may have one glass with a meal, say at a wedding or other function.'

She always tries to have biscuits in the house, to offer to visitors with a cuppa. 'But you can bet an unexpected visitor always turns up on the very day you don't have any. That used to be a bit embarrassing when I was still working in a biscuit factory.

'I used to like Carr's Sports biscuits and another one called Lunch. A shame they are no longer made. As a youngster I also used to like Blue Riband and Nice biscuits. Butter sultana cookies were another favourite. I bought them in Marks & Spencer when I was sent as a girl into town on a Saturday, along with such delights as angel cake, date and walnut cake and of course the cookies. These were for tea on a Sunday. As a child I didn't like fig rolls.

'My biscuit-eating habits have changed over the years. I don't eat as many as in my younger days, but I do like a "luxury" biscuit like for instance a triple Belgian choc cookie.

'When I was first working at Carr's, we did sometimes eat the biscuits, especially if you were in the chocolate room. But the novelty soon wore off and you just did your job. Nowadays you are definitely not allowed to eat any of the products.

'I used to like working on small Table Water Biscuits, in the days when you hand-fed the biscuits into a measured slot, ready to be wrapped. Today they're gravity-fed automatically.

'There weren't really any biscuits I didn't like working with, but both custard and Bourbon creams are notoriously difficult to slot feed when temperatures are high, particularly in the summer months.

'Working at Carr's certainly did not put me off eating biscuits. We used to be able to buy cheap broken or reject biscuits from the works shop, which was a good benefit when the children were young. They and their friends were always looking for a biscuit and often there would be a crowd of them at the back door. We also used to get a selection of biscuits both sweet and savoury as part of our Christmas present. But I don't think they get anything these days.'

Although her cancer is in remission, Barbara still has backache and sore arms and wrists, a legacy of her working life.

'The pains won't go away now, after twenty years lifting biscuit boxes, but I don't blame Carr's. It's what women have to put up with, if we do those sort of jobs. When we are young we think we can cope, but women are not generally as physically strong as men, whatever we might think.

'I remember when I first started at Carr's standing for an hour stacking boxes on to pallets – each containing thirty packets of biscuits weighing four kilos. And there was a bloke beside me, just standing there with his empty barrow, waiting for me till I'd finished so he could take it away. That still happens – but now they mostly have electric barrows, so there's little physical work for the men. But women do still have it hard when they do any sort of factory work, despite some of the new automatic machinery.

'But all jobs have their problems. Carpet fitters get terrible knees, typists get repetitive strain injuries.

I look at all these kids today living on their mobile phones and computers. I am sure they will suffer for it.

'On the whole, though, I enjoyed the work, apart from the last couple of years. I loved the lasses and the company – but most of all I was grateful for the money. We ended up with somewhere nice to live and we have three cars, just for the two of us, which I know is extravagant. Dave does like his cars. He's still got a Jag, but that's just for weekends. And we've got personalised number plates. He also has a Fiesta to get him to work, while I have a Focus.'

Barbara doesn't think she deprived her two children in any way by having worked so hard these last thirty-two years. 'I saw them all day, when I was on evenings, and Dave looked after them otherwise. And they did always get the latest Nike trainers.

'We should end up having some extra money in the bank, when we buy the smaller place. In fact I am going today to the solicitor's office to pick up the cheque for the sale of our property.

'In the end, of course, property doesn't mean much, it's just a possession, but it is good to have something nice. I have seen many a nice council house, that's been done up, so you would never know its history. At the end of the day, though, one's health and family are far more important.

'When I think back, there have been lots of happy

times in my life. In fact overall I am lucky and consider I have had a good and happy life.

'I was really happy when I passed my Eleven Plus and gained a place at Carlisle and County High School – probably even happier when the reward was a new bike. I was equally happy when my mother trusted me enough to let me give up that high school place some three or four years later to transfer to the local secondary school to pursue a business studies course – on condition that I still did my O levels.

'Other highlights included an exchange trip with a French student and many family holidays in the south of England in Devon, Cornwall and Norfolk. Meeting and marrying my husband and having my two children are also highlights.

'Another highlight was a flying lesson given for my fortieth birthday. I actually got to fly the plane over our house, needless to say this was the first and last time I took control of a plane.

'There of course have been a number of low times throughout my lifetime. My first real bereavement was probably that of my grandad Sammy who was a real character with a twinkle in his eye and a wicked sense of humour. He died in 1973 aged seventy-eight I think, just a week or two after his golden wedding anniversary. My grandmother who was seventy-three at the time lived for a further nineteen years and passed away in 2002 at the great age of 102.

'My mum died in 2001, she was only sixty-nine, and is greatly missed by us all. She was a major influence in all our lives and always instilled into us the need to work hard if you wanted to achieve your goals. She used to say "you don't get owt for nowt in this life".'

'When my son was about nine years old he was taken into hospital and diagnosed with meningitis. It was a very worrying time for us all, but he was lucky – it was viral meningitis and not the much more serious bacterial meningitis. There was no treatment, the virus just had to burn itself out.

'Another low point of course was the breast cancer diagnosis at the age of fifty-two. But feeling sorry for yourself never got anything done. I soon realised that I would just have to get on with it, have the operation, do the chemotherapy and radiotherapy and then go back to work. That sounds so easy but it definitely is not. But my approach to all things has always been deal with it and then move forward.

'It does of course alter your perspective on things and your priorities change. After being back at work for about two years and having turned fifty-five I decided it was no longer a priority of mine to work and the main thing was to live my life doing what I wanted to do each day and not doing what I thought I had to do. It sounded selfish but deep down I had to do what I wanted for myself. Luckily I was in a position where

I was able to leave employment. Many people can't afford to give up work.

'As a girl, I was fairly quiet and reserved and probably still am. I was probably also a bit on the shy side and just got on with things and basically did as I was told and aimed to please where I could, keeping my opinions in the main to myself. This was in a bid to stay out of the spotlight and not attract any negative attention.

'Over the years, though, I have gained much more self-confidence. I am not afraid to voice an opinion or put across a contentious point of view. I do appreciate that everyone thinks differently and has different views and opinions about pretty much everything. It would after all be pretty darn boring if we all thought the same.

'I don't really worry about the future, or what will happen to me. I have never been a worrier. I always say what will be will be. Another thing I say is that I don't have energy to waste worrying about what might be. I just deal with what comes along.

'We have spent the last forty years building a home and providing the best we could for ourselves and our children, with the children almost always taking priority. We have now decided after great deliberation that in the future we should be the main priority. Our remaining time should be for us first, while always being there for the children and grandchildren. My main aims for the future are to make lifestyle changes that will enable David to retire at least a couple of years earlier than his state pension date, so that we can spend more time together doing the things that we enjoy, like more trips out at the weekend and longer holidays abroad, especially in the winter months. So, all going well, the future, however long that may be, looks to be as exciting, as fruitful and as rewarding as our life so far. So you see I don't personally really want much – just a happy and comfortable future.

'I think working women and career women generally have it easier today. We didn't have maternity leave and assisted nursery places like they do now. We had to make our own arrangements, either pay for help or get someone in the family to look after the kids.

'You see young lasses today dumping their kids at school early in the morning, long before it opens, shoving them into the Breakfast Club, then they are in the After School Club. They can hardly see them. A sign of the times we now live in, I suppose. Even though I worked so hard and for so long, I like to think my own children always had their breakfast at home, and their tea.

'I always had a fear of ending up as a pensioner with no money, like some of the older generation.

'So, I have to admit, Carr's has served me well.'

Chapter 21
Ann

Ann in 2013

Ann continued to juggle work as a union convenor and the demands of being a single mother. For a time she was joined at Carr's by Adrian, her son. He had gone into the local metal box factory when he left school, and then joined Carr's for a short period, thus becoming the fourth generation of Ann's family to work there.

He was still the apple of his grandmother's eye. She had looked after him after school during those years when Ann had been on the evening shift. Eventually, Adrian settled down with a partner, rented a council house and had children of his own. He still visited his gran a lot, and of course his mother Ann.

In his early teens, Adrian did have some drug-related problems, and spent some time at a young offenders' home. Ann hoped it was a passing phase, and blamed the drug culture of the times. It was particularly serious on the Raffles estate, the estate which had once been a model of social housing but by the 1990s had become drug infested, with dealers operating openly, houses boarded up, gardens left overgrown, old cars dumped in front hedges, and people scared to go out at night. For a time, Raffles featured as one of the most deprived estates in the whole of England.

A report in the *Independent on Sunday* newspaper in April 1994 described the estate as a 'no-go area with a high level of crime' and quoted one resident as saying, 'If you've got a problem in Raffles, get a shotgun.'

One Thursday in 2001, Ann went with Adrian and his three young children to Chester Zoo for the day. They all had a great time. A photo of them taken that day shows them all smiley and happy. Adrian looks well, his hair brushed forward in a schoolboy fringe, like a latter-day Beatle. He appears healthy if a bit thin and incredibly young-looking to have three children.

Two days later, on the Saturday, Ann was shopping at B & Q in Carlisle with her younger brother when his mobile rang. It was his wife, asking them to come to Ann's mother's house at once.

'When I got there, the police had gone. My mam was distraught, so I feared the worse.'

Adrian had been found dead after an overdose of heroin. He was twenty-seven.

Ann arranged the funeral service at the crematorium. Many of his friends turned up. Ann wanted nothing to be hidden, the causes of Adrian's death to be known, as a warning to all.

'People thought druggies were all emaciated, down and outs, but they are not. I honestly saw no signs in Adrian at Chester Zoo on the Thursday that he was back on drugs. But it's an addiction and hard to escape, especially if someone supplies you. Looking back now, I think if he had been born earlier or later it might not have happened. He was born at the wrong time, a time when drugs were rife in the community he was living in. I wanted his death to be warning to those in his group.'

She found a retired vicar to give the address – which she wrote. Today she has it framed in an italic script, like a medieval manuscript.

Adrian died because he took drugs
I have lost my son because of drugs
My parents have lost a grandson because of drugs
His three children have lost their father because
of drugs
I have family and friends grieving for me because
of drugs
I am so angry that myself and all these people

Have been put through this terrible time because
  of drugs

I am not that naïve that saying this will
Stop everybody from using drugs, but if it only
Makes a few think about all the pain and sorrow
It brings to themselves and their family
Adrian's death will not have been such a waste

Adrian is free of it all now and so are his family
But oh what a price we have had to pay
He was all I had and drugs took him away
  from me
I have peace of mind but I have no son
GOD BLESS YOU, SON, SLEEP WELL

At work, Ann threw herself into her activities as the union convenor, going to meetings, in the factory and elsewhere in the United Biscuits group, sorting out problems.

The Carlisle flood drama of 2005 at the Carr's factory was a traumatic time for Ann, in her union role, just as much as for the management, worried about getting production started again.

'It broke my heart when I walked through the Bourbon department the day after. There was water everywhere, tons of muck, massive tins of biscuits just floating around. I thought they'll never clear this up. We've had it now. Almost two hundred years of history down the drain.

'At that time, the Ashby de la Zouch factory had recently been closed, so we were all worried we would be next.

'But we all mucked in, came in and helped out. There were a few moans from some of the ones who were called in to work, to help clean everywhere up, while those at home were getting paid but doing nothing. But that was just a few. I have to say that everyone was kept on full pay during the three months the factory was closed. It was a miracle that it all opened again – and so quickly. Perhaps the closure of Ashby had helped us. Perhaps they didn't want to close another factory so soon, so that's why they rushed to get us open again.'

In reality, the vital factor, according to the management, was the fact that they had excellent insurance cover, unlike many of Carlisle's ordinary domestic householders. They were able to access the insurance money and start clearing up and rebuilding very quickly. Being part of United Biscuits, a large modern, well-run conglomerate, definitely paid off in this instance.

So Ann and the other shop stewards, along with all the workers and management, were soon able to get back to normal, with production increasing, more lines coming on, and the firm doing well once again.

*

In 2008, after ten years as the factory convenor, Ann went one day into a shop stewards' regular meeting. During the meeting, one steward happened to ask her if she was in the management's pocket. Ann thought, that's it, I've had enough.

'I resigned there and then. I hadn't intended to. I hadn't gone into the meeting with that in my mind. It was all in the heat of the moment, but I thought no, I really have had enough.'

Ann remained a Carr's worker, despite resigning from her union position, as she was still employed by them. In some cases, convenors have often gone on to management or personnel positions. Ann found herself being offered a job as learning coordinator for the factory.

This was a scheme that had come in under the Labour government: one of those idealistic schemes that for a while the country could afford. The idea was that in each factory there should be a learning place, a room set aside with computers, materials, tools and instruments, where ordinary workers could learn new skills, if they wanted to. Not in company time, but after work. All funded by the government.

'The scheme was union-led, paid for by the government, but we got the backing of the company, which was vital. They really helped and encouraged it, seeing it as a training tool.

'One of the things we did was to help people read and write. The government at the time was worried people were masking that they couldn't read, not letting on, so we helped them to come forward, keeping it confidential. So we did a lot of good. You could also learn computer skills. We also helped people to write their CVs. At one time we had a lot of Polish workers, brought over when we had staff shortages. They were very keen on learning to read and write English.

'Anyway, the scheme came to an end – and the company lost interest. That's what companies do. They like things when they are free, paid for by the government, but afterwards they lose interest. When they have to pay, they suddenly don't want to know.'

The scheme finished in December 2012, when the funding ran out. Ann then finally and officially retired, aged sixty-three. The last of her family, after four generations, to have been a Carr's worker. Perhaps the last ever to work there.

Since her retirement, Ann has still been involved with Carr's, organising the pensioners' club and their Christmas party on a voluntary basis.

She would like to see an annual works outing making a return, the sort of thing which Carr's did so splendidly up until the war, when the whole factory went on fete to Silloth or Blackpool, had a beanfeast, enjoyed activities and entertainment, all paid for by the company.

She discovered, in her days as a convenor and visiting other factories in the group, that some of them have resurrected the idea and introduced fun days – an annual event, usually in the factory, with partners and children invited, rather than an outing to the seaside. She hopes they will return to the Carr's factory. The present management does seem keen on implementing a modern version.

Ann lives alone, in her own nicely converted and extended ex-council house. She never married or found another serious partner.

She enjoys cooking, and, unlike some of the others, has moved with the times. 'Today I love pasta, rice, love cooking Indian and Chinese. But I suppose really that my favourite is still Sunday roast. Oh, and I do like a glass of wine – or two.

'My parents always voted Labour. I have always made the effort to vote, but I don't think a lot of any of the politicians today. One party always blames the other's policies.

'Looking back, I did have lots of happy times when I was young with family and friends. And I loved being a hairdresser. As a teenager I was quite shy and a bit of a worrier. The biggest change in my life came with working at Carr's, going on to do the union job. I gained a lot of confidence.

'Today, I do love being a nana to my three grandchildren, Adrian's children. They are now eighteen, seventeen and fifteen. I babysat them when they were younger. As they got older, they stayed at weekends and I took them on holidays.

'The lowest points in my life have been losing my son, and also my parents. I do worry about what age will bring, especially the thought of anyone having to live with someone with vascular dementia. My father had it. It's like a stroke of the brain. It's terrible watching loved ones slipping away from you. He didn't get it till he was eighty-six and then he died at eighty-nine. So he just had it for three years. My mother died at ninety, so I suppose I have good genes. But I don't want any of my family to have to go through what I did with my father, when my time comes.'

Chapter 22
Ivy

Ivy in 2013

Ivy, the oldest of our biscuit girls, has now been retired for twenty years, since that day she travelled down to the London headquarters in 1993 to get her long-service award for forty-five years.

'Earlier on I had had a presentation in Carlisle, at the factory, when I got to fifteen years and then thirty years' service. The thirty years one was held in the canteen and about fifty people were there. I wore a dress. The factory director, Mr Crowther, shouted out the names and all the long-service people went up, one by one. My friend Gladys Wright thought she was going to be the last to be called, as her name begins with a W, but it was done in reverse order and she was first.

'Mr Crowther shook my hand and thanked me for all my years of service. I was very happy. You felt part of a happy family. I got given a gold watch, so that was nice. For my fifteenth I got a voucher, which I stupidly spent on a costume. I should have saved the money.'

For her final retirement event, after forty-five years, she travelled to London and got a cheque for £1,000 from the chairman.

'I also got two presents from my friends at Carr's. One was a white fish, china of course, not real. This was because they had all heard my joke about one of the fish in the factory fishpond – which is still there – the one I had said had been named after me.

'The other was a kitchen stool. I thought I'd not let on about that, as I had been told to keep the man's name secret, but obviously over the years folks had heard about that stupid mistake I had made, all those years ago.'

She moved, some twenty years ago, from the council house in Dalton Avenue, Raffles, where she had lived with her mother, to a two-bedroom council house at Belah, on the other side of the town, considered a nicer area than Raffles.

However, in the last few years, Raffles has at last begun to come up. Since 2004 around £10 million has been spent on redevelopment, knocking down many of the drug-ridden, crime-infested old 1930s council houses and building bright new attractive more spacious houses on tree-lined streets. Could Raffles become a desirable place to live once more, as it was back in the 1930s when Ivy was born and her parents were so excited to have secured such an up-to-date new house?

Ivy lives alone, except for Winky, her blue budgerigar. 'I love him to bits. I did think of getting a parrot, but decided against it. A parrot wouldn't get a word in. I talk all the time, even just to myself.'

The house and the garden is immaculate, the lawns and hedges neatly clipped, all done by Ivy herself, even at the age of eighty. Unlike most of her other colleagues, all those years of hard labour have clearly not affected her health and strength. She has to take some blood pressure pills, but that is about all. She always appears cheerful, ready to laugh, make jokes.

Ivy had to learn to cook having done none as a girl or young woman. 'When I was working, my mother still made all my meals for me, but when she fell ill, I had to take over and learn what do to, making a meal for us all when I came home from work. I just made what she had made – meat and two veg. Oxo pie was one I liked making.

'I still cook for myself – and cook the same old things I ate when I was young. I never buy ready meals, apart from fish and chips. I couldn't be doing with things like pasta or oil. I shop at Morrisons and when I go up town

I go into Routledges for bread and rolls and Cranstons for meat and pies. I don't drink wine, never have done. Don't like it. If I am out somewhere, and I have to have a drink, I might have a port and lemon. I quite like it.'

Three out of our six biscuit girls have suffered some sort of ill health, before or during their retirement. Fairly normal on the whole for their age. But it is noticeable that the three most outwardly healthy and fit are Ivy, Dorothy and Ann, none of whom got married, though Ann did have a son.

Ivy had just had her thick white hair cut short, almost a crew cut, flat on top, rather modern.

'I dyed it once when I was young, just with shampoo, and it was a disaster. If it was a special occasion, I would go to the Co-Op and have it permed. But mostly I have always kept it short and tidy. That's how I prefer it.'

She has never been much of a follower of fashion. Most fads passed her by. 'I did wear nylons when they came in. I remember the New Look, just after the war, and everyone talking about it, but all it seemed to be was that coats were longer than normal. I did buy one and I got used to it.'

She loved Elvis, and still does, but also liked going to concerts by the Carlisle Music Society and trips to Blackpool to see the big variety shows.

In her childhood, they got several newspapers at home, but today she doesn't read any daily or Sunday newspapers, except the local one, the evening paper, the *Evening News*. 'I buy it two or three times a week when I am up the town. I used to buy the *Cumberland News* on a Friday but it's too heavy for me to carry.

'I'm not really a reader. I never joined a library, even as a child. I once went along to the library in town, Tullie House, with a friend after school but the lady was so nasty it put me off libraries for life.'

Ivy has no interest in politics and never votes. 'My parents did vote. I remember them going to Newtown School to cast their votes on election day. They always voted Labour. I think politicians today don't know what they're doing. They are always arguing. They should be fair with people but they just seem to be in it for themselves, only interested in themselves. No, none of them have done anything for me.'

Apart from her TV, which she has on much of the time, she doesn't have much truck with modern technology. She doesn't have a computer or use a mobile, and she has long given up her little car now she is on a fixed income.

Some neighbours assume that after all those years at Carr's she must have a good pension – but she never contributed to a pension scheme till her final years. Her state pension comes to around £100 a week, while her Carr's pension is slightly less. Her total income each week is £200 – but she reckons it costs her £300 a week to live. Her council rent is £90, then there is council tax, plus heating, lighting, food and other expenses.

She is therefore living on her savings, which she put into a building society during her last years at Carr's, along with a small sum when she took her pension.

'I hope there's enough left to see me through, then that's it. But don't you worry yourself – you can have a ham tea at my funeral...'

In the last ten years she has started travelling – usually on an Irving's coach from Carlisle, on an all-inclusive holiday, with people she knows, usually to Devon or Cornwall.

She went abroad to Canada with a friend for the first time a few years ago.

'Well, she wasn't a close friend, just someone I knew. She was going with someone who dropped out at the last moment and I heard myself saying, "I'll go with you." But it didn't work out well. That taught me a lesson.'

She did later go on another foreign holiday, to the Algarve, with a younger woman with whom she used to work, who always refers to Ivy as Aunty. She invited Ivy along, with her own family – and it turned out a big success.

More recently Ivy had been on a train excursion – a day trip to Oban in Scotland. 'I just saw it advertised in the paper and thought that would suit me champion. I was about four hours on the train there, four hours back. I only had two hours in Oban, but I loved it. I might do it again. I think I've now got up the courage to travel alone on the train.'

She usually has some sort of biscuit in the house, mostly rich tea and Kit Kat or any other sort of chocolate wafer biscuit. 'I always have a biscuit after my evening meal, not during the afternoon. After I've eaten, I like a nice cup of tea and a biscuit to finish it off.

'I never buy Carr's water biscuits. I never liked them. But they're good for diabetics. Miss Spence, who was my boss in personnel, and then went on to do something in the cathedral when she retired, she was big in the church, she used to eat baked water biscuits. She was diabetic.

'I once had one of the high-ups from London come to visit me at home, from personnel. I wanted to give her a nice biscuit with a cup of tea, so I went out and bought some Kit Kats. "Why have you not got Carr's biscuits?" she said. She never let me forget that.

'At work, when I was working on the line, I used to try all the different biscuits, though you were not supposed to. I would pop one in my mouth when no one was looking. I liked chocolate tea cakes and Sports biscuits, they were my favourites. I don't know why they stopped making Sports biscuits. They were lovely. I said this once to one of the bosses. He never said anything. I said you're missing out there.

'I also liked the cheese crisps, they were lovely as well, but I never liked celery biscuits. I don't know why they made them. Nobody seemed to like them, but they didn't do them for long. Garlic water biscuits, ugh, I didn't like them either. I don't like garlic.

'I loved the Victoria tins of biscuits – they were all chocolate. You can still get them, I think. You would open the lid and be disappointed if you couldn't immediately see your favourites.

'One of my jobs when I was in personnel was to go round the pensioners at Christmas and they each got a Victoria box of biscuits. Some years the staff all got a box of biscuits as well, but towards the end of my time I think they stopped that.

'We were allowed to buy tins of broken biscuits quite cheaply. If they gave you them in an old tin, you couldn't take it back, but if you got them in a new tin you could take it back and get money. Just after the war there was still a tin shortage so there was a deposit on them. I think you got one and six back on a new tin.'

Ivy goes most weeks to a coffee morning at the local church, but never goes to church itself, though they are often asking her.

'I was never sent to Sunday school, like most of my schoolfriends, because my mother was not religious either. In my own heart, I think I am religious, but I think I get more out of going to Carlisle cemetery than I would from going to church. I go most weeks to tend the graves of my mother and father. I cut the grass, make it look nice, and sit for a bit and remember them.'

Carlisle cemetery, on the south side of the town, with the main entrance in Richardson Street, dates back to 1855 and is a classic Victorian cemetery, covering thirty-eight hectares, with chapels, ancient and impressive gravestones, but also hills, woods, little rivers and bridges. The main stream through the cemetery is known as the Fairy Beck. There are wild orchids, wild violets, butterflies, dragonflies and a variety of small mammals. It was one of the first cemeteries in the UK to introduce woodland burials, which have minimal impact on the environment, the graves being marked by an oak tree. In 2008 it was named the UK's cemetery of the year for the third year running. People visit it, just to visit, as it is like a large nature reserve, studded with Victorian monuments. You can easily get lost in it, with all the hills and trees. From the end of the cemetery, there is a clear view of the Caldbeck Fells and the Lake District mountains.

Behind it, further down Dalston Road, is the crematorium, which is much more modern and more like a municipal park. This is where Dorothy's parents are buried, and is the one she visits.

It now takes Ivy two buses to get right across town to the old cemetery, but she thinks it is worth it and an interesting outing in itself.

'I get off at the Dalston Road bus stop and walk down Richardson Street to the main entrance. I always love going. When I had the car, I used to take a lawn mower with me, putting it in the boot, an old-fashioned hand mower which you pushed. Nowadays, when I have the energy, I carry a pair of shears in a plastic bag, but I now find them a bit heavy to trail all that way. I go through the main entrance, over the bridge, then I turn left through the woods. And there they are, my mother and father, both in the same grave. I suppose I'll end up there as well.

'I suppose it was the unhappiest time in my life, when my mother passed away. Apart from that, I tend only to have good memories. I was always happy as a child, with my parents and my brother. We seemed to have such fun times, especially going to Silloth on the train.

'At school I was happy as well. Though I was always very shy and nervous when I was younger. At primary school I could never have been in the choir as I was far too embarrassed. But I got better as I got a bit older, as a teenager. I was so proud when I was chosen to go and get the milk for the teachers. I had to collect it from Messenger's Farm at Morton Manor, where Sir Robert Chance used to live, then bring it back to school.

'Today, I do speak up for myself, if I have to. I like to think I treat people as I liked to be treated myself.

'But I do worry of course what will happen when I get poorly and I can't manage to do things for myself. I do wonder who is going to look after me...'

She has two nephews, now grown up, the sons of her brother Tommy, who died in 2012 aged eighty-five. They are her only blood relations.

'I have chosen the hymns for my funeral, but I haven't made a will. Why should I? I have nothing to leave. No house, no property, not even my car as that has gone. But it doesn't worry me.

'I always assumed I would get married, but it didn't happen. No one asked me. I suppose it was because I was never pretty enough. I also have quite a big mouth, and say what I think. Then of course I spent a long time nursing my mother till she died. But I don't regret not being married. It doesn't bother me.

'If I had got married, I would have been a widow by now, I'm sure of it. Women outlive men, don't they? So I would now be on my own anyway.

'I am quite happy in my little house, as long as I've got my health and strength.

'I often think I am probably a pleasanter person, not having been married. You come across a lot of people unhappy in their marriage. And you get all these women who have been abused. No one has abused me. I have always felt strong.

'I do feel I have had a good life. No complaints, no regrets. I never asked for things but I think I did get a lot in the end. It was hard, mind, for many years, hard physically. I wouldn't like to do some of those jobs again. Not that I could, at my age. But the last years in personnel, going out visiting people – that was lovely.

'So yes, overall I loved working at Carr's. And yes, I would do it all again.'

Afterword
Carr's Today

The main sign at the entrance to the factory says McVitie's, which is what it is officially called today, so technically you should never call it Carr's. But look high up on the main building and you will see there is a large logo with the word Carr's and an image of the famous water biscuits. The good people of Carlisle can therefore justify continuing to call it Carr's. And probably always will, as long as it is there.

It still plays a large part in the life of the town – and in the life of women. The day of my visit – in July 2013 – the wife of the current Mayor of Carlisle was a Carr's employee, Cath Wilson, a supervisor in assortments.

The building is large, commanding, the tallest and most impressive in that part of Caldewgate, but a bit of a hodgepodge. The entrance building beside the main gate is low and cheap and modern, like a petrol station forecourt. Then there are some nondescript botch-job structures from the 1960s round to the side.

As you leave the entrance area, having gone through the various passport controls and East European-type barriers, that's if you happen to have arrived in a car, there is a little fountain and ornamental pond, easy to miss as it could do with a clean. But I had a quick look, just in case Ivy's fish was still swimming around, the one supposedly named after her. No sign of it, though.

Behind, across a yard, is a vast prison-like structure, the archetypal Victorian factory building. On a good day, and Carlisle does get them, and in clear light, it can seem handsomely austere, almost as grand and imposing as Carlisle's nine-hundred-year-old castle, just a few hundred yards away, through what were once the old gates into the city.

Above my head as I went through the main gates were an assortment of seagulls making a terrifying screeching sound as they swooped down, like cries of help mingled with cries of rage and vengeance. You forget, while in the middle of Carlisle, just how near it is the sea – though on the map, it appears to be right on the Solway Firth.

The factory employs a hawk to keep the seagulls away. They are of course vermin whose droppings could easily poison a million Bourbon biscuits in one fell swoop.

Getting into the factory proper was harder and took longer than getting through Heathrow airport. Apart from the endless security checks, you have to get kitted out. All visitors to the factory areas, like all workers at whatever level, even the manager herself, have to wear a white overall, black clunky safety shoes and a mob hat made of some gauze-like material. The staff hats are blue. Visitors wear red.

A notice above a wooden box announced 'Beard Snoods'. I thought of that fashion among footballers a few years ago for wearing woolly snoods in the winter to keep their precious necks warm. I stopped smiling when I was ordered to wear one. Beard Snoods are for moustaches as well as beards. They have to be covered up in case of, well, I was not sure why, my moustache is incredibly clean I hardly spill anything on it. I wondered how the rabbis cope, with their full head of facial hair, when they visit the factory. The reason, of course, is to prevent any hairs getting into the biscuits.

Rabbinical inspections are still made, as they have been since 1910, in fact they had been the day before and I had just missed them. Matzos, the special Passover unleavened bread, are no longer produced at Carr's, but all their small Table Water Biscuits are declared kosher, a rabbi coming up from Manchester every six weeks to make sure all the ingredients conform with their rules, and that no traces of seafood, pork, rabbit or any other forbidden items have crept into the process. On each packet there is a symbol to show it is kosher – a large U inside an O, which stands for Orthodox Union.

I was in sandals and bare feet that day, as Carlisle was tropical, which meant I had to wear the safety shoes with no socks. As I clunked round the factory, my feet got heavier and more uncomfortable, as if I was space walking. But the worst part was my moustache snood. I could hardly breathe in it.

The first production lines I came to, Bourbon biscuits, seemed much as I had imagined them – probably much as the production lines had been back in the 1840s. Rows of silent women, working away. But there was one surprise. Background music, pounding out on all the production lines from CFN Radio, a local commercial station. None of the biscuit girls had mentioned that. Apparently it has only been introduced in recent years. Let's hope it does not inhibit all the chatting among the lasses.

The girls on the Bourbons were concentrating hard, unsmiling, getting on with the job, endlessly picking up twenty Bourbons at a time from the millions flooding towards them down the tracks, then feeding them into wrapping machines, just as they have done for decades.

There seemed to be an enormous wastage of Bourbons that day, with the waste bins at the end of the line filled to capacity. The unusually tropical weather was not allowing all the chocolate cream to set as it should. But there is no real waste, my guide stressed. All the offending biscuits get recycled.

In the creamery area there was another compulsory safety measure: ear plugs. Everyone has to wear them, workers and visitors. Presumably they don't want people suing for loss of hearing.

As we did our tour, Christine, my guide, proudly pointed out two areas where they had recently spent small fortunes – £5 million in all – installing robots. Unlike the Bourbons, the ginger nut department is now automatic. Giant hands now pick up ginger nut biscuits and speed them on their way. So no need for as many women packing ginger nuts.

The other robot area is one that is making life easier for the male workers. Most of the man-powered barrows and heavy wooden pallets have been replaced by robots which lift up the heavy tins and send them for what seems like miles around the factory on a miniature railway line, plonking them straight into the delivery wagons. The result is that there are no warehouses, no biscuits at all remain on the site, they are whisked straight away, off to the four corners of the world. The factory still works round the clock, with three shifts of eight hours, but almost every biscuit leaves the factory the same day, zooming off the minute a shift is finished.

The bakehouse has eight ovens. They are still mainly run by men, as in the old days. The ovens are enormously low and long, stretching about two hundred feet, much as that Dalston schoolgirl described them in 1948. They sit like rows and rows of squatting, interconnected dishwashers, through which the dough passes in minutes, and comes out baked.

On all the production lines I saw, in all the departments, except the two robot areas which appeared empty of humans, it still mostly appeared to be women workers. Their average age seemed to be in their fifties, and they were stocky and sturdy and confident. The handful of younger girls working among them looked thin and worried by comparison. Perhaps they were new. As Barbara said, if you can last to your first pay packet, you've cracked it.

One of the women who had cracked it was Angela Gibbs, the current manager of Carr's and only the second female manager in the history of the factory, whom I joined for lunch in the canteen after my tour.

She comes from Barnsley, took a degree in engineering at Aston University, worked in various firms, including Quaker Oats and Gillette, before joining United Biscuits in their Leicestershire factory. She was promoted to Carlisle in 2010 – a much bigger site, producing 84,000 tons of biscuits a year as opposed to 18,000 tons at Leicester.

That day, when I visited, there were 665 on the permanent payroll, with another hundred on temporary contracts hired through an agency. Depending on the season and the demand, such as coming up to Christmas, they normally have between 100 and 250 extra agency workers. So today there is a total of around 800 workers at any one time, around half of whom are women.

Ten years ago they were having recruitment problems, sending some of their personnel people to Portugal, Poland and elsewhere to hire more staff.

Their recruitment problems today are mainly to do with attracting and retaining young staff. They also have a high absentee rate – with 6 per cent being off at any one time. They do have a relatively old age profile – and of course they always did, as traditionally Carr's workers stayed on for decades. Young girls today, says Angela, would like money and fame, so it's hard to recruit them. Many do disappear on the first day, after their first break.

The hope is to make the job more attractive, getting away from the 'cracker packer' image, stressing all the new automated machinery, calling the workers 'technical operators' or ATMs, which stands for Advanced Team Member. They hope that offering sexy-sounding jobs working with the robots will appeal more than standing on a production line sorting biscuits by hand.

The main products today at the Carlisle factory are ginger nuts, seven million being made each day, followed by six million Bourbon biscuits and six million custard creams. Over the year, around twenty different types of biscuits are produced. A new one recently introduced is Flat Bread, an oblong cracker, a bit like a Ryvita.

Water biscuits are not made in the quantities they once were – and most of them are exported, the Carr's name still being recognised all round the world among biscuit eaters. They make small water biscuits and also flavoured ones – garlic, sesame seed and black pepper. Only the savoury biscuits, as they call their various water biscuits, carry the imprint of the Carr's name on the biscuits and the packaging. With all their other biscuits, such as the Bourbons, the Carr's name does not appear.

I then learned some dreadful news, which I had not been aware of. It had somehow not made the London papers. Two years ago, Carr's lost their Royal Warrant for their water biscuits, an honour they have had since Jonathan Dodgson Carr achieved it in 1841. The Royal Household, apparently, no longer uses them. It has made little difference to sales, so Angela maintained. Instead of the royal coat of arms on the packets they now have the equally impressive Carlisle city coat of arms.

Over the last ten years, total production at the factory has doubled, from 40,000 tons annually to 80,000, but times are still tough, thanks to the recession, the cost of raw materials like wheat and flour going up all the time and also the intense competition in the biscuit world, from rivals such as Fox's biscuits. But Angela was convinced the future was bright, that the Carr's factory was the best in the United Biscuits group, that production would keep going up.

As well as the Carlisle factory, United Biscuits has six sites today in the UK, with another six around the world, notably in Holland, France, Belgium and Ireland. Their best-known brands include McVitie's, Carr's, Jacob's, Penguin, Jaffa Cakes and Mini Cheddars. They also make cakes, and have done so for many royal weddings, including Prince William's. United Biscuits are the biggest biscuit manufacturers in the UK – and probably the second biggest in the world (exact ownership of some of the American companies is hard to pin down). Overall, they employ 6,700 staff, 5,000 of them in the UK

It is remarkable that production on the Carlisle site, while not employing as many as it did in the heyday of the Carr family back in the 1920s and 1930s when the staff reached 3,000, has managed to survive and compete and increase during these last three decades when so many biscuit factories, and much of British industry itself, has suffered from competition from the East and elsewhere. At the Carr's factory, they like to think it is because they are producing a premium product and running an efficient, modern factory.

Angela had recently introduced a modern version of the old time annual outing, which disappeared after the war. Ann would approve. In February, the factory closes for a day and all the workers – shift by shift, i.e., three hundred or so at a time – go off in coaches from the front gates to a restaurant, the White Heather Hotel, about ten miles away, out in the country. It is technically an employee briefing, not strictly a jolly, and in the morning they get regaled with the state of the factory, objects and achievements, are encouraged to work hard and keep up production, but they do get to enjoy a free two-course meal and in the afternoon have some sort of entertainment or a quiz.

They also have introduced a staff magazine, *McViews*, but alas it is nowhere new as handsome, comprehensive, informative and fun-filled as the old *Topper Off*. I picked up a copy, just four pages, and it appeared not to have any personal contributions from staff but was filled with management speak on things like compliance training and hitting key targets.

It is unfair to romanticise the good old days when the Carr family was in charge, having that personal touch, being nice to the workers, putting welfare before profits, in theory anyway. It was far more dangerous, uncomfortable and back-breaking than it is today.

As I came away, pleased to get off my clinging, cloying uniform and clunking shoes and let my moustache have some fresh air, I had to admit that the factory as a whole was nowhere as hot and noisy as I had expected. It was more spacious, with high, airy ceilings, no crowding or clutter or nasty-looking objects lying around. The working conditions are as comfortable as can be expected.

For most of the women, despite the odd robot, the actual work is just as repetitive and physically wearing as it has ever been. How could people like Ivy, and all the Ivies before her, and all the workers who have ever worked on factory production lines in our long and glorious industrial history, have survived doing such jobs, hour after hour, day after day, for up to forty-five years? Necessity is the answer.

I could now fully understand why Ivy had painted such a glowing picture of sitting in that country cottage that day when she was visiting a sick colleague – and thinking how lucky she was. Compared with life back on the factory floor, she was indeed in heaven.

The thing about factory floor jobs is that there is no escape. White-collar workers can find some way of skiving, wandering off round the building with bits of paper, or higher up they can go to meetings, conferences, enjoy jollies, freebies, hotels, visits abroad. On the production line, you are stuck, trapped, just another cog in the process.

Installing more robots in all departments will presumably come one day, which will turn our biscuit girls into historical figures, living lives we can no longer comprehend or believe, so it is worthwhile to record and acknowledge them now, should they turn out to be the last of their breed.

But they won't be, not quite, not in the immediate future. United Biscuits, or whoever controls the Carr's factory in the next few years, are unlikely to be able to afford or justify the investment of robots on all the production lines. Not if the present economic climate continues.

One of the interesting and rather touching things about our six biscuit girls is that they all felt they had enjoyed their time at Carr's, especially working with other women, and did not really blame the factory for any aches, pains or illness some of them later suffered.

All six of them did keep on working until a retirement age, survived until they were able to take their pension, and mostly they managed to enjoy some well-deserved comfort in their retirement years.

As I write now, in June 2014, Dulcie has sadly just died. Let's hope the others have more years to come, able to think back fondly, perhaps even with pride, to the long years they gave to Carr's and to what they consider to have been happy but hard-working lives.

Acknowledgements

Books

There is still no standard book on the general history of biscuits, which is surprising, considering their importance in our social and economic history, so anyone hungry for biscuit information has to track down histories of individual companies, some of which were published privately and consequently hard to find, or books on the history of the Quakers, which usually have a section on biscuits.

I relied heavily for the history of Carr's on the truly excellent and entirely wonderful book by Margaret Forster, *Rich Desserts and Captain's Thin: A Family and Their Times, 1831–1931*, published by Chatto & Windus, 1998.

Also valuable was: *A Fell Fine Baker: The Story of United Biscuits* by James S. Adam, published privately by Hutchinson Benham, 1974; and *The Quaker Enterprise in Biscuits* by David Burns Windsor, Muller, 1980.

I read innumerable books about the history of Carlisle and found the best for my purposes included *Carlisle: An Illustrated History* by D.R. Perriam, Bookcase, 1992; *Carlisle* by Sidney Towill, Phillimore and Co,

1991; *Industry in Carlisle*, written and published by A.D. George, 1994; *Old Towns and Cities: Carlisle* by Kenneth Smith, Dalesman, 1970.

Guide to Carlisle was published by Carr's in 1902, ostensibly a guide to the city, but contains interesting illustrations and material about the Carr's factory. Carr's also published a useful booklet 'The Story of Carr's Biscuits' in 1951.

Jolly amusing to read was *Nice Cup of Tea and a Sit Down* by Nicey and Wifey, Time Warner, 2004, and very informative was *Biscuit Tins* by Tracy Dolphin, Shire Library, 2011.

People

I would like to thank Stephen White, local studies librarian at the Carlisle Library for all his help digging out references and cuttings and books, and particularly for making available all the copies of the *Topper Off*, the Carr's staff magazine which ran between 1928 and 1964.

Also helpful was Edwin Rutherford, social history curator, at Tullie House – particularly for the opportunity to listen to and read – for most have been transcribed – their oral history collection. Both the Eric Wallace memoirs (Chapter 2) and Miss Raven's (Chapter 10) came from this source.

A thank you to Nigel Slater for support, food historian Ivan Day for advice and Angela Gibbs, Jane

Davie and Ian Beattie of the present-day management of McVitie's biscuit factory in Carlisle for their time and help.

Ann Mullholland's assistance was invaluable – introducing me to the Carr's pensioners' club and enabling me to meet our heroines.

But most of all, obviously, how could the book have been done without them, so a huge thanks to Ivy, Dulcie, Dorothy, Jean, Ann and Barbara.

Appendix 1

Carr's Biscuits 1860s

A list of Carr's biscuits available during the 1860s and later. Many of the names, reflecting the fashions, social, economic and political times, have long gone, but some of the names are still recognisable today.

Abbotsford
Abernethy
African
Albert
Albion
Almond
    " Bread
    " Drop
    " Finger
    " Ring
American Crackers
Anneau
Artic
Arrowroot Cakes
    " Plain
    " Thin
    " Rich

Balmoral
Bath
Beaufort
Boudoir
Boulevard
Bouquet
Britannia
Brunswick

Butter
Button Nuts

Cabin
Café
Captains, thin
Caricature
Cashmere
Castle
Celebrities
Ceylon
Charm
Charivari
Cheapside
Cheese
Chocolate Drops
Citizen
Clarence
Cocoa Nut
    " Finger
College
Colonial
Combination or
    people's mixed
    (25 variety)
Cornflour

Coronet
Costume
Cracknell
    " Cup
    " Dessert
    " Fancy
Cream Crackers
Croquet
Croquette

Demi Lune
Digestive

Eclaire
Eclipse
Epine
European Mixed

Fingers, plain

Gala
Garibaldi
Gem
Gem, iced
Gingerbread,
superior finger

Ginger Buttons
Ginger Nuts
    "   "   Finger
Glace
Grantham

Heraldic
Hominy
Honey Cakes

Ice Creams
Iced Rings
Iced Rout
Imperial Fruit
International

Java

Kennel
Kent
Kindergarten

Leger
Lemon
    "   Drops
    "   Fingers
    "   Nuts
    "   Rings
Lunch
Lunch, small

Macaroons
Madeira
Marguerite
Marie
Menagerie
Metropolitan Mixed
Midget
Mignon
Milk

Milk Crackers
Minaret
Minerva
Mixed (25 varieties)
Mixed Nuts

Naples
Nic Nac
Noblesse, or cherry
    macaroon
Nursery

Orange Drops
    "   Fingers
    "   Squares
Oriental
Osborne
Oswego Cakes
Oxford
Oyster Crackers

Pain D'Amandes,
    or almond bread
Parkin
People's Mixed
    (25 varieties)
Picnic
Pocket
Popular
Prince of Wales

Queen's Drops

Ratafias
Regent
Rice Cakes
Rich Dessert
    (20 varieties)
    "   Seed
Riviera

Rose
Royal
Rusks
    "   Finger

Savoy
School
Scotch Oaten
Scrolls
Shells
Shrewsbury
Small Change
Smyrna
Social
Soda
Sponge Rusks
Star
Stella
    "   Plain
Sugar Wafers
Surrey
Swiss Drops

Table
Target
Tea
Town

Urania

Victoria Drops
    "   Nuts
    "   Finger

Walnuts
Water
Wheaten
Wreath

Appendix 2

Carr's Biscuits 2014

Carr's of Carlisle is now part of United Biscuits and the factory is officially known as McVitie's, but the Carr's name continues locally and appears on some packaging.

United Biscuits is the biggest biscuit manufacturer in the UK. They have seven factories – in Carlisle, Hayes in London, Halifax, Wigston in Leicestershire, Tollcross in Glasgow, Aintree in Liverpool and Stockport, Manchester.

Their main brand names, several of which go back to the early nineteenth century, still appear on many of their biscuits and on the packaging. Apart from Carr's, they include Jacobs, McVitie's, Crawford. Most of the factories produce a wide range of biscuits, many making 'own brand' for the supermarkets.

This is a list of the biscuits currently being produced by the Carlisle factory – not all carry the Carr's name on the packaging, though the savoury ones do, such as the Carr's Table Water biscuits.

Assortments
Bourbon Creams
Cheese Melts
Coconut Rings
Cookies including Boasters, Hobnobs and Tasties
Custard Creams
Digestives
Flatbreads
Fruit Shortcake
Ginger Lemon Crèmes
Ginger Nuts
Gold Bars
High Bake Water
Minipacks
Morning Coffee
Nice
Oyster Crackers
Rich Tea Finger
Shortcake
Shorties
Small Table Water Biscuits, including sesame, garlic and herb and black pepper